The people who matter most in our lives are like lighthouses: we can count on them to stay sturdy through a storm and shine a path to guide us through darkness. Steve Pemberton shows us how to find them—and how to become them.

ADAM GRANT, #1 *New York Times* bestselling author of *Think Again* and host of the TED podcast *WorkLife*

If you have ever doubted whether your work impacts the world, *The Lighthouse Effect* is for you.

MILDRED JOYNER, president of National Association of Social Workers

Steve Pemberton has done it again. The stories shared in *The Lighthouse Effect* left an indelible mark on my heart. The visualization of the moments in the lives of these extraordinary people awakened in me the power of human connection and the realization that a lifeline of caring can provide a beacon of hope.

ROSE BOWMAN, principal of Old Hammondtown School and Steve Pemberton's second grade teacher

The Lighthouse Effect is perhaps most of all an exercise in daily gratitude for the power of small moments—and the people that make them happen.

ERIC MOSLEY, CEO of Workhuman and coauthor of *Making Work Human*

The
LIGHTHOUSE
EFFECT

The
LIGHTHOUSE
EFFECT

HOW ORDINARY PEOPLE CAN HAVE AN
EXTRAORDINARY IMPACT IN THE WORLD

Steve Pemberton

ZONDERVAN
BOOKS

ZONDERVAN BOOKS

The Lighthouse Effect
Copyright © 2021 by Stephen J. Pemberton

Requests for information should be addressed to:
Zondervan, *3900 Sparks Dr. SE, Grand Rapids, Michigan 49546*

Zondervan titles may be purchased in bulk for educational, business, fundraising, or sales promotional use. For information, please email SpecialMarkets@Zondervan.com.

ISBN 978-0-310-36234-0 (audio)

Library of Congress Cataloging-in-Publication Data

Names: Pemberton, Steve, 1967 June 15- author.
Title: The lighthouse effect : how ordinary people can have an extraordinary impact in the world / Steve Pemberton.
Description: Grand Rapids : Zondervan, 2021. | Includes bibliographical references. | Summary: "Our culture is adrift in division and distrust, and we need everyday heroes more than ever. Drawing from his own remarkable journey, Steve Pemberton shares stories of the ordinary people who quietly change lives and bring change to their communities. Compelling and insightful, this book will inspire you and renew your hope for the future"— Provided by publisher.
Identifiers: LCCN 2021008830 (print) | LCCN 2021008831 (ebook) | ISBN 9780310362326 (hardcover) | ISBN 9780310362333 (ebook)
Subjects: LCSH: Conduct of life. | Virtues. | Mentoring.
Classification: LCC BJ1547.4 .P46 2021 (print) | LCC BJ1547.4 (ebook) | DDC 158.1—dc23
LC record available at https://lccn.loc.gov/2021008830
LC ebook record available at https://lccn.loc.gov/2021008831

All Scripture quotations are taken from The Holy Bible, New International Version®, NIV®. Copyright © 1973, 1978, 1984, 2011 by Biblica, Inc.® Used by permission of Zondervan. All rights reserved worldwide. www.Zondervan.com. The "NIV" and "New International Version" are trademarks registered in the United States Patent and Trademark Office by Biblica, Inc.®

Any internet addresses (websites, blogs, etc.) and telephone numbers in this book are offered as a resource. They are not intended in any way to be or imply an endorsement by Zondervan, nor does Zondervan vouch for the content of these sites and numbers for the life of this book.

Cover design: Curt Diepenhorst
Cover image: John Lund / Getty Images
Interior design: Sara Colley

Printed in the United States of America

21 22 23 24 25 26 27 28 29 30 /LSC/ 12 11 10 9 8 7 6 5 4 3 2 1

To John Sykes
For the light you were and the light you remain

CONTENTS

Preface xi

Introduction xv

1. John Sykes 1
2. RJ 25
3. FL Kirby 47
4. Greg Anthony..73
5. Rick Rock 99
6. Carmen Ortiz-McGhee.. 115
7. Welles Remy Crowther.. 143
8. Monica Kachru and Rajeev Tipnis 161
9. Claire Levin.. 179
10. Setting Your Sail for Home............................... 199

Acknowledgments...203
Notes 205

PREFACE

I have found it is the small things. Everyday deeds of ordinary folk that keeps the darkness at bay. Simple acts of kindness and love.
—GANDALF THE GREY, *THE HOBBIT: AN UNEXPECTED JOURNEY*

I did not have high expectations for my first book, *A Chance in the World*. The truth is that none were necessary. Its purpose, I believed at the time, was to serve as a family history that future generations would pull down from a dusty shelf and read one day, should they ever be so inclined.

Soon it became apparent, from those who sought me out, that in the course of sharing my own coming-of-age journey, I had managed also to write chapters of other people's lives. The very first response I received was from a seventy-three-year-old Irishman who wrote to share that he too had experienced great losses in his childhood, but because of what I had written, he could now go to his final rest in peace.

In another part of the world, a young mother from a remote African village shared that she had read my book to her young children as an example of the importance of perseverance.

When we share our life stories, we invite others to share their own and in so doing offer ourselves a chance to find a common narrative, a more unifying story of family, faith, fortitude, and forgiveness that transcends distance and difference.

Hearing those stories is what inspired me to write this book.

The lighthouse is a perfect symbol for what I have learned from others' lives. In a flat world, the lighthouse is the tallest structure in the sea; set amid this alternatingly peaceful and turbulent environment, the lighthouse is noble, selfless, steady, and faithful. It requires no recognition and seeks no reward. Rarely will you see a name on a lighthouse; its identifying features are found in its beautiful and poetic design. The lighthouse does not judge or ask how the traveler has come to be in danger; after all, it finds itself in the same storm. Neither does it concern itself with socioeconomic status or the political party to which the voyager might belong. The lighthouse has but one mission: to protect the journey of the traveler.

We need the symbolism of the lighthouse now more than ever. In the film *The Lord of the Rings: The Two Towers*, Samwise Gamgee paints a vivid picture of the great need for these timeless structures.

How could the world go back to the way it was when so much bad has happened? But in the end, it's only a passing thing, this shadow. Even darkness must pass. A new day will come. And when the sun shines it will shine out the clearer. Those were the stories that stayed with you. That meant something, even if you were too young to understand why. . . . Folks in those stories had lots of chances of turning back but they didn't, because they were holding on to something—that there's still some good in this world and it's worth fighting for.[1]

The need to find goodness, to believe that all will be well, to find some virtue in the land, is a perpetual yearning of humanity. This desire sends us searching for heroes, looking upward to celebrities, kings, presidents, executives, or anyone seemingly above us to offer us guidance and direction. The elevated hero is often placed in front of us as an example of that which we should aspire to. But I have learned that another kind of heroism exists. It is found in the lives of the seemingly ordinary people who live alongside us, their unpresuming lives often unknown, ever valuable because of what we can learn from them. Having an impact on the world is not reserved just for those who have the means and the visibility to do so. The stories of everyday heroes are the ones I have been drawn to, and these are the stories that will unfold in these pages.

These humble individuals' life journeys will take us from the harsh battlefields of Vietnam to the famed Los Angeles Dodgers clubhouse, from a wonderful love story beginning in the beautiful land of New Delhi, India, and an unlikely father-daughter reunion in Puerto Rico to a quiet Father's Day in a rural farmhouse in Wisconsin. You will meet those who have turned personal pain into possibilities for themselves and those around them. Together we will learn what motivates them, where their compassion comes from, and the lessons their lives can offer us. In the process, we will harken back to our own human lighthouses, those who saw our possibilities, and in the process be reminded of the power—and the responsibility—we have to be the same. Though the stories are from different generations, races, genders, and faiths, these individuals share a common denominator: *the lighthouse effect.*

In illuminating the pathway to safety, the lighthouse offers us a chance to move beyond the fears and uncertainty of the storm and toward the peace and calm of safe harbor. So it is with the people who most impact our lives. For while lighthouses of the sea have stood watch for millennia, the most powerful and enduring lighthouses are the human ones.

Steve Pemberton

INTRODUCTION

The dip of the light meant that the island itself was always left in darkness. A lighthouse is for others; powerless to illuminate the space closest to it.

—M. L. STEDMAN

A magnificent battleship was at exercise in dark and stormy weather. The proud captain, neatly attired and adorned with medals, was standing on the bridge issuing commands and surveying the performance of his crew. The ship's lookout, whose job was to be aware of danger, suddenly spotted a light from another ship on the starboard side. He informed the captain of the threat, to which the captain asked, "Is the light steady, or is it moving?"

"Steady, captain," came the emotionless reply.

Keenly aware that the two ships were on a collision course, the captain ordered the lookout to send the other ship the following message: "Change course twenty degrees. We are on a collision course."

The message from the other ship came back: "It is advisable for you to change course."

The unwavering captain sent back a terse message: "I am a decorated captain with over twenty-five years of experience in the United States Navy. Change course twenty degrees."

Back came a second reply: "I am two months away from earning my Coast Guard license. You are the one who needs to change course twenty degrees."

The captain, now furious, sent his reply: "This is a fifty-thousand-ton battleship. You will not survive a collision. For the last time, change course!"

A long pause ensued before the final message came back: "I am a lighthouse. It's your decision."

In the interest of full disclosure, this tale did not actually happen. Yet I find this old maritime joke an appropriate description of how we view leadership and success. From an early age, we are taught that heroes and leaders are a lot like the captain of the battleship—strong, mighty, decorated, and absolutely certain of their course. It is an idea born of a confidence in legacy and training, emboldened by advancing technology that appears to bend nature to its will, furthered by a laser-like focus on the destination and a relentless and unyielding belief in their ability to lead. We celebrate these individuals and point *up* to them as an example of what leadership looks like—and what we should be. But it is a short walk from these rightly admired qualities to entitlement, arrogance, and hubris.

Unfortunately, those characteristics also seem to attract attention in our world today, blurring the line between the infamous and the authentic hero. Attracting attention, regardless of the way it is achieved, seems to be an end unto itself. We are not wrong to look for heroes, but we often look in the wrong places, only to find ourselves continually disappointed. Against the great wall of heroism, we place the wrong ladders and give too much credence to those we put on the pedestal. The dazzling entertainer, the elite athlete, and the innovative CEO do have admirable qualities, but we can't place them so far above us that we fail to see our own ability to make important contributions to the world.

More recently, another kind of culture has emerged from this need for adulation, less noble in its intent than our seafaring captain's. Cynicism, polarization, and division have become the denominators of our world and our interactions. It appears the most important factor we want to know about someone is the label we believe tells their story: their race, gender, occupation, or political affiliation. Value is derived by whom we can cancel, condemn, or criticize. By any measure, societies across the world are more divided than in any other time in recent memory. Each day we wake up amid one conflict or another, and we often gawk at the spectacle, alternatingly fascinated, entertained, and alarmed, but seemingly powerless to change it. Goodness seems to be the exception and not the rule.

This division has led us to no good place. Our world is not made better or stronger. The damaging effects of this

I-culture are all around us. We have descended into warring clans isolated by a culture of voluntary segregation that has left us more anxious and uncertain, unable to respond to the great challenges of our time. It is no accident that massive social protests unfolded amid an unrelenting global pandemic that has taken over three million lives and fundamentally altered our way of life.

Social media, in its best form, should offer us a different way. But it has not. What was intended to further connect the world has devolved into a hostile environment of immediate judgment, self-absorption, and negativity. In this echo chamber of edited lives and false perceptions, where likes, retweets, and followers are the currency, attention is what matters above everything else, no matter how it is obtained.

In our desperate search for solutions, we often turn to the world of public service, but our present-day political culture offers no resolution. The current nature of our political discourse is rooted in opposition so deep it allows no room for understanding or healing. Polarization, the kind that destroys everything it touches, is the price we pay. Working across the aisle, coming together for the greater good, seem to be nothing more than nostalgic notions of a bygone era, even though the founding fathers wove the spirit of compromise into our political system. Too many of our public servants are deeply immersed in a culture of me-first and me-only, craving power and attention, and have a greater loyalty to their own ambition than they do to preserving, and yet still improving, our systems and traditions.

The election of one party appears to ignite backlash from the other party, who immediately begin plotting how to seize power again. Value appears to be derived from what one can stop, rather than who you can serve. To say this is just politics rings hollow when truth, principle, equity, and morality are often casualties in this political world that bears no resemblance to the way most of us live our lives. This climate of political polarization, aided and abetted by a media business model that values spectacle above all else, will solve nothing. It never has. All it can offer us is further fracturing, deteriorating society into a thousand clans with a thousand causes and leading us to forget the magnificent truth of progress: it is best achieved together.

Like many others, I have grown weary of the division and dissonance and long for a way forward. I too question whether we are able to see how much this destructive path has already changed our national character. I quietly wonder whether we can summon the will to find our common story, to disrupt the idea that our differences—and our fears—are too big to overcome. I, like many of you, want to know that all is not lost, that despite it all, we can find a common good in our land.

And we can.

There is another force far quieter, more humble, less celebrated, and anchored solely in a greater good that can give us hope again. It will allow us to feel good about the world again, to affirm that goodness, to be connected to it, to see it in ourselves as well as in others. In the end, it is not just a guiding force but the greater one.

How I Came to the Idea of the Human Lighthouse

In the world of Kindle, there is a feature called "popular highlights." Readers—and authors—are able to see which passages are most highlighted. In *A Chance in the World*, the most popular passage is this one: "[Audiences would tell me] I did not look like my story. I would respond by saying that none of us really do; it is impossible to tell, from a single glance, the journeys that someone has traveled, the experiences that have made them who they are."[1]

In the years since the book's publication, this lesson—that none of us look like our stories—has become even clearer to me.

When I thought about what book I would write next, I was unsure of the topic. I only knew that I did not want to write a sequel to my own story. While I appreciated the widespread support and am grateful for the book's impact, there was nothing new for me to add. As it turned out, the subject I was looking for had always been right in front of me.

Over the years, I have heard many personal stories, from middle-school children and their teachers to corporate executives and retirees, from places as far away as Australia and as close as my hometown of New Bedford, Massachusetts. I have heard them through social media and at conferences, from longtime friends and complete strangers. I never tire of these narratives. It is quite an honor to be deemed worthy to hear these stories, for people to share an important part of their lives with me and for me to learn I have inspired them in some way.

When we hear these stories, we see deeper into humanity. We come to understand how people walk through the world, the great joys of their lives and the quiet regrets they harbor. We see the pains they hold on to, the secrets they carry, and the dreams they are trying to fulfill. We grasp their great losses and their great loves. We witness sacrifice we can barely describe and strength and resilience we didn't think human beings could possibly possess.

Human stories connect us because they let us know we are not alone—either in our joy or our suffering. If we can better understand one another's stories and find those mutual chapters of tragedy and triumph, we can reconnect a world that often seems lost in its own storm.

The United States Lighthouse Society is a treasure trove of information about lighthouses. A visit to their website will tell you the first known lighthouse was the Pharos of Alexandria, Egypt, built by Ptolemy I and his son Ptolemy II between 300 and 280 BC. (This is why lighthouse enthusiasts are referred to as "pharologists.") You'd learn the tallest functioning lighthouse in the US, standing at 198 feet, resides at Cape Hatteras, North Carolina, and the oldest surviving lighthouse in the world is the Tower of Hercules watching over the North Atlantic coast of Spain. You'd come to know that Alcatraz Island housed the first lighthouse on the West Coast of the US and the Statue of Liberty once operated as a lighthouse.

There are 22,900 lighthouses across the world, yet no two are exactly alike.[2] This is not an accident. Each lighthouse has its own distinct markings to make it more recognizable to navigators. These patterns of colors and shapes, known as daymarks, also make it easy to distinguish one tower from another. The height of the lighthouse, essential to its visibility, is partly determined by the natural elements of the earth. A lighthouse built on a soaring cliff, like the breathtaking Tasman Island lighthouse of Australia, need not be as tall as the stunning Jeddah Light of Saudi Arabia, which seems to rise, phoenixlike, from the depths of the sea.

There is a certain bravery that defines the lighthouse. The beautiful symmetry of this marvel, and its alignment with nature's landscape, is breathtaking but misleading, for it disguises the treacherous location where the lighthouse resides. Wherever you see a lighthouse, danger almost certainly lurks. Yet this fearless structure stands in quiet defiance, dwelling where danger lives, and warns us not to come toward it but to move away from it, as if to say, "That way!"

For all their diversity, architectural beauty, and in more recent times, technological capabilities, lighthouses today have many structural commonalities. Each is round, dispersing the power of the violent winds and waves of the sea, bending them around the curves of the lighthouse. Atop the tower stands the signal beacon; in ancient times this signal was a fire, and today it is a powerful lens. The room housing the beacon is a glass-paned lantern room, and beneath it is the gallery deck, a steel platform encircling the tower. The highest point of the lighthouse is the lightning rod, intended to deflect the powerful bolts of electricity that frequently strike lighthouses.

One of the peculiarities of the lighthouse is the radius of the powerful light that emanates from its tower. Most of the light in our daily life illuminates the area immediately around us. But as novelist M. L. Stedman points out, the lighthouse has a different purpose. It is designed to project outward, to be seen from a distance rather than up close.

The greatest and most common factor of every lighthouse lies in its purpose. Since the beginning of time, its mission has been the same—guide the journey of the traveler. The lighthouse fulfills its mission by directing, protecting, and correcting our travels. Strategically located at the entrance to a harbor or bay, it serves as an important navigational aid. For adventurous sailors of the past, the sudden appearance of the lighthouse on the horizon signaled the final stage of the journey—and its most dangerous. The lighthouse warns seafarers of shoals, dangerous reefs, and prior shipwrecks, which could mean disaster, whether at the beginning or the end of the journey. (As a young boy growing up in a historic whaling community, I remember seeing photos of the *Wanderer*, a New Bedford whaling ship whose final voyage ended before it began when it was blown onto a shoal by hurricane winds.) Should dense fog reduce visibility, the lighthouse has its own song, in the form of horns, bells, and cannons, to warn sailors.

The architectural magnificence of the lighthouse masks that this structure is built to be resilient. It must be, for it exists in a beautiful yet brutally unforgiving world. Humans can never conquer the sea; they can only hope to coexist. The presence of the lighthouse acknowledges this fact, particularly in the midst of a raging storm. No matter how beautiful the lighthouse appears from a distance, a closer look reveals the many scars from its never-ending battle with the sea.

To be caught in a powerful storm at sea is a terrifying experience. Relentless swells of violent water pound your vessel. The world is windy, gray, and misty. A fast-moving, roaring skyscraper of seawater approaches, and suddenly the bow of the ship points straight toward the heavens. For a moment you are certain the boat will capsize, but then in another instant your world drops vertically, and you wonder if you are headed straight to Atlantis. But miraculously you emerge intact. You begin to celebrate your good fortune, but then you see another mountain of water approaching—and this one is bigger than the last.

It is during the storm that the guiding mission of the lighthouse is fully on display. You can see it off in the distance through the dark sleet, the cloudy mist, and the doubt that has crept into your mind. It is not the structure itself you can see but the powerful light emanating from the lantern room. You're thankful the refracted light, visible from miles away, has replaced lamps, which were far less powerful. The lighthouse, the savior of the sea, beckons you toward safety.

It has been debated as to whether lighthouses are still necessary. Concessions to technology have long been a way of life in the lighthouse world. Most lighthouses are now automated, and so lighthouse keepers, those once responsible for taking care of the lighthouse and who lived in isolation, are almost obsolete. Additional technologies such as electronic navigational charts and global positioning systems are more useful tools than the lamps and lights of yesteryear. For navigating the sea, the lighthouse serves as little more than a backup to modern navigational tools.

Yet the lighthouse endures. In 2000 the United States Congress enacted The National Historic Preservation Act to create a process for the transfer of federally owned lighthouses into private hands. This legislation, an extension of a prior law, is intended to place these monuments of the sea into the hands of those who want to preserve them. August 7 is National Lighthouse Day in the US, when citizens are encouraged to visit lighthouses and donate to support their preservation.

These ageless monuments, one of the last reminders of a world without electricity, will still be with us. We often preserve history because it connects past and present, a reminder of where we are and where we once were. The lighthouse offers us something further—a powerful reminder for how we might live, how we, in our seemingly ordinariness, can bring calm to a world of chaos and uncertainty.

The human lighthouse is a beacon, someone offering us hope and inspiration and guiding our journey. The purpose of this book is to share with you the stories of those human lighthouses I have met along the way. I encountered them at different stages in my life: as a young boy, as a new father, or well into my professional life. We met in the course of everyday life: going to school, riding on a train, attending a conference, or playing a round of golf. They are, at first glance, seemingly ordinary people going about their daily routines, but a closer look reveals that they are a lot more.

If you have picked up this book expecting to read about the wealthy or the famous, you will be disappointed. In all candor, I have had my fill of celebrity culture and the genuflecting idolatry that accompanies it. I am not inclined to participate in the grandiosity of it all. Rather, these individuals aren't particularly well-known. They don't have massive social media followings. You won't see them on the evening news or on a movie screen. No crowds cheer their names. Their value is not measured by material successes, individual wealth, worldwide attention, or public approval.

Though I came to know a lot about these people, I didn't ask them where they worship or whom they might vote for in the next election. I wasn't interested in comparing their stories, for each story exists in its own time and place. Nor did I concern myself with each person's race or gender or whether I agree with them on a particular social issue. To do so would have confined them to the narrow margins, when they can offer us so much more. The lessons of these lives are deeper and greater, their examples enlightening, useful, and ever necessary in a world that sometimes loses its way. To move beyond this age of rancor and polarization, we need to put our ladders of hope against different walls and to make room on the pedestal of heroism for these human lighthouses.

Human lighthouses are steadfast and faithful, humble yet unwavering, always illuminating the pathway to hope and sanctuary. They summon us to a better understanding of ourselves and point us all toward a greater humanity.

Their view of the world is not born of a naive idealism, for each faced adversity that could have broken them. Yet they show us how to move forward, how to heal, and how to find meaning. I came to understand that their positive impact in the world is *because* of the challenges they endured, the deep principles they hold, and a universal belief that others might benefit from the challenges they encountered.

In the midst of my own bustling, they made me pause to reflect on their examples of strength, conviction, courage, and selflessness. And I believe they will do the same for you.

CHAPTER 1

JOHN SYKES

I got you to look after me, and you got
me to look after you, and that's why.
—JOHN STEINBECK, *OF MICE AND MEN*

It had been a long day, and for the last several hours, I
had been intensely focused on my social worker's body
language. Mike Silvia had been flipping through a green
loose-leaf notebook, going down a list of names and calling
telephone numbers. Those he could get on the phone would
listen to his request, politely decline, and wish him happy
holidays. He'd gently hang up the phone, sigh ever so slightly
so as not to show his frustration, and glance down the hallway before going back to the notebook to call another name.

As daylight turned to dusk, there seemed to be a never-
ending stream of phone clicks, sighs, and looks down the
holiday-decorated hall. "They don't know what to do with

me," I thought. It was a familiar feeling. I'd entered the foster care system at the age of three, taken away from my mother, who had been in a losing battle with alcoholism, two weeks before Christmas. I would never see her again. What followed was a nomadic journey from one foster family to another, largely because there wasn't a manual for what to do with a biracial boy who had been labeled as damaged goods. Finally, at the age of five, a few weeks after my father's murder, I was placed with a family that had taken in foster children for many years and had been frequently recognized for their efforts.

But it was all a ruse. Taking me in was a way to add to their monthly income while sentencing me to a childhood of servitude. The foster parents dwelled in manipulation and guile and were masterful at deceiving teachers and social workers. They made it clear that I was to be a participant in their scheme because "troubled kids like you go missing all the time and nobody ever asks any questions." Hunger, isolation, and beatings were their tools of instilling fear in me as well as ensuring my silence. They were just as effective at exploiting the foster care system. Reading was my only escape, which in turn made me a good student and ultimately allowed me to set my sights toward attending college—and escaping the foster family once and for all.

For the last eleven years, they had thwarted every effort I made to find a better world. But when they threatened to do the same with my dream of going to college, I took a stand, improbably navigating the complex foster care system to secure my release. Now just three days after Christmas, I desperately needed a miracle: a place to stay for the night.

To deal with the anxiety of not knowing where I would go, I paced around the empty office, walking past cubicles filled with photos of families on vacation. That was a foreign world to me. Somewhere in the office, holiday music played. My wandering took me in the direction where Mike had been looking. My question as to what was down the hallway was answered when I saw a couch in an empty office. Was he thinking I could sleep there tonight?

I came and sat back at the desk where Mike had just hung up the phone. His sigh, more audible this time, told me he was out of options. "Do you know anyone you could stay with for a few days?" Mike asked. "Friends? Anyone?"

My immediate thought had been no. I'd been socially isolated since I'd been in the foster home. I simply didn't have the friendships most sixteen-year-olds have. But then I remembered a conversation I'd overheard a high school counselor, John Sykes, having with one of his colleagues: "I don't have any children. But if I did, I sure hope they would be a lot like Steve." Like many children who have endured multiple foster homes, I doubted I had any value to offer the world. The idea that this might not be true was hard for me to believe.

"Hey, Mike . . ." I summarized the conversation I'd overheard outside the counseling office. He perked up with interest. "Can't hurt to try," he said, picking up the phone. "John Sykes, you said his name is?" I nodded.

The call was a long shot if there ever was one. First, it was winter break and teachers and counselors were not at school or in their offices. Second, even if we did reach him, there was little possibility he'd let me stay with him for a few days. Holidays are a time to be with family, not to take in stray teenagers, I reasoned. At best, Mike could leave a message. While it still didn't answer the question of where I would sleep that night, at least it was something.

Mike dialed John's office fully expecting to leave a message, but he didn't need to. John was in his office finishing up some paperwork. After a brief conversation, John agreed to the arrangement: I would come stay with him until the start of the new year while Mike worked to find me a more permanent placement.

As Mike and I drove toward John's office, I thought a bit more about where I was headed or, better yet, to *whom*. John Sykes was the most popular teacher and counselor in the Upward Bound program. Focused on helping first-generation college students negotiate the college admissions process, the program was staffed by passionate educators and led by a real-life angel in Margery "Ruby" Dottin.

Much of the reason for John's popularity was because he struck us as an older version of a teenager. Witty, mischievous, and passionate about literature, he seemed to live life in quiet rebellion, wearing his hair long, riding Harley-Davidsons, and humming the tunes to his favorite country music songs. For a bunch of city kids, he was equally fascinating and mysterious.

Mike and I pulled into the parking lot near John's office. The last vestiges of light were barely visible on the empty college campus. John strolled down the campus walkway, backpack slung low over his shoulder, as if he didn't have a care in the world. He and Mike exchanged handshakes and talked quietly while I grabbed a green garbage bag out of

Mike's pickup truck. It held all my worldly belongings. As they spoke, I warmed my hands with my breath, barely able to comprehend that I was finally free.

John and Mike interrupted my trance to inform me that I would be able to stay with John until the beginning of the new year. I thanked Mike again and wished him a happy new year. John and I got into his weathered green Volvo and took the short drive to his home, a small cottage not far from Horseneck Beach in Westport, Massachusetts. When we pulled into his gravelly driveway, the sound of the crunching stone informed me I was in a completely different world than where I'd been. If I doubted that, a glance down the single-lane country road where no houses could be seen made the point. It was incredibly quiet save for the sound of crickets. But none of that bothered me because, for the first time in my life, I was free.

John's only spare room contained a large bar and small desk and wasn't going to serve as a bedroom on that first night. Our solution was to drag up from the basement an old dusty cot with broken legs. Duct tape made it functional again. John grabbed a spare blanket from his bedroom closet and asked me to test out my makeshift bed in the living room. "Actually, wait," he said, plopping down onto the cot. The cot groaned but did not break. "That'll work," he declared.

As the first few weeks of the new year unfolded, finding me a home had become nearly impossible. One night, John and Mike sat me down to explain the situation and propose a solution: if I was willing, I could stay with John for my last year and a half of high school. They'd have to do background checks on John first and complete some paperwork, but assuming everything panned out, I could plan on staying there until I headed off to college.

I was relieved. Those long hours in Mike's office had a sobering impact, for I was keenly aware I had no options left. So while I enjoyed my temporary placement, my long-term situation had been weighing on me. Now in an extraordinary act of kindness, John had opened his home and his heart to someone he barely knew.

Soon we settled into a routine. One of those routines was having dinner at a small kitchen table just big enough for the two of us. Cooking was not John's forte, and our meals often consisted of microwaved chicken croquettes and instant mashed potatoes. Here at the table, we talked a lot about our favorite books (mine was Richard Adams's *Watership Down*, and his was John Steinbeck's *Of Mice and Men*), our mutual love of literature, world issues, and the future, specifically my future.

For years my foster family told me I was worthless. "Nobody wants you, including your own parents" was a common refrain. Sitting in my social worker's office watching his frustration as he couldn't place me was further proof of that. Rejection had been a constant way of life. The young man who arrived at John Sykes's cottage was one filled with doubts.

But John had a plan. In his mind, if you were going to defeat doubt, then you had to take some gambles, and he was insistent I do so, as long as I was informed and prepared. Still I would hesitate to take on these risks, wondering whether I could truly succeed. Each time he would insist that success was not the point, it was the willingness to take the leap that mattered. Soon I was taking Advanced Placement English and excelling on the high school track team.

Whenever I tried to thank him for encouraging me, he would wave me away. "It really isn't that hard," he'd say. "You like to read and you run like a jackrabbit." John's "jump and figure it out on the way down" philosophy was most on display when it came to realizing my biggest goal: gaining admission to my dream school, Boston College. The biggest obstacle standing in my way was the cost of tuition.

John explained that the best way for me to afford college was to apply for scholarships. When I asked him how to apply for these scholarships, he sent me on a mission to the college counseling office. I returned to the small dinner table with my prize—an enormous book of scholarships—and jokingly announced I was going to apply for a scholarship for left-handers.

"But you're not left-handed, Steve," John pointed out, taking a bite of his grilled cheese.

"I'm not, but I betcha I could learn." I grinned.

With a slightly mischievous grin, he asked to see the book, and thus began a dramatic exercise of flipping through the pages. Finally, he circled one particular scholarship. He slid the book across the table to me. "That one," he said, repeatedly tapping his finger on the page for emphasis. "You really should apply for this one."

I looked at the title and started laughing. "No chance."

"How do you know?" he asked, raising an eyebrow.

"Because it says right there it's for Daughters of the American Revolution," I said in protest, pointing to the page. "You do know I'm a boy, right?"

He chuckled. "I kinda figured that out already. But let me ask you this. Does it say you *shouldn't* apply?"

I looked at the description. "No, it doesn't."

"Then you should apply," he offered, shrugging his shoulders as if this were as simple as one plus one.

My tone turned a bit more serious. "You know they're going to reject me." What I didn't say was that I'd already had enough rejection to last a lifetime and wasn't keen to have yet another experience.

"Maybe," John replied. "But then again, maybe not."

I let out an audible sigh, not attempting to disguise my frustration.

John put his fork down. "Think about what you're trying to do here. On the one hand, you're trying to attend one of the top schools in the country. On the other hand, you might have to experience some rejection or denial to get there." He held his hands up, palms facing the sky, as if they were two scales. "Rejection on one hand, possible acceptance to a great school on the other hand." He paused for a moment. "The risk is definitely worth the reward."

After more discussion, it became clear he was not going to let this go. I reconciled myself to applying for the scholarship, knowing when my rejection letter arrived, I would at least have the satisfaction of being correct. My plan worked—until I showed John my rejection letter when it arrived several weeks later. He quickly scanned the letter and handed it back. "They must have made a mistake. I guess you are going to have to write them back."

"And say what exactly?"

"Ask them if they are sure."

I thought about protesting, but I already knew John wasn't going to change his mind. Ultimately, I did write back to Daughters of the Revolution and asked if they were sure about their decision. They replied again in a tone that said, "We are really sure, so please don't write us anymore." John knew I was going to be denied, of course. But he also knew something I did not: I was going to be told yes by many more, which is how I managed to find my way to Boston College after all—on a full scholarship no less.

Over the years, I've thought a lot about that last-gasp phone call that cold December day and our many conversations at the small kitchen table in the tiny cottage. The more time has passed, the more improbable, if not miraculous, it all seems. As I came to understand John's story, the improbability of it all was even greater than I knew.

John Sykes grew up in Fairhaven, Massachusetts. His dad, a second-generation American of English descent, worked at Atlas Tack Corporation, just down the road from his childhood home. His mother, a first-generation American by way of Portugal, was a stay-at-home mom. He remembers quite fondly his years growing up in a safe neighborhood, so safe that his mother often left young John on the porch step alone while she tended to the laundry and other chores.

One day she returned to find him gone. She called the police, who started looking for him. There were no amber alerts or missing person reports back then. Four-year-old

John had simply walked a mile down the road to Fort Phoenix, an American Revolutionary War fort, now a state park located at the entrance to the New Bedford–Fairhaven harbor. The police found him there sitting on the rocks, looking out toward the ocean, much like you might find him today. His memory from the day was not one of fear but the joy of working the police siren on the way back home.

It was a simpler time in America. The country had emerged victorious from World War II because of the sacrifices of the Greatest Generation, the brave men and women who stewarded America through some of her greatest difficulties. John's father had done his part to secure America's freedom, having fought in Africa and Sicily.

John's childhood years included walking to meet his dad, who walked home from work each day at suppertime. He recalls fondly his attempts at impressing his dad with his nearly nonexistent whistling skills. John's dad would always ask him to try, though young John could never do it and honestly still can't. Even so, his dad would encourage him to give it his best effort, and no matter what sound escaped John's young lips, his whistle was always good enough for his dad.

When John's little brother Jimmy was born, the family moved to New Bedford to be near his grandparents. His mom got a job at the local bank, and John would walk home from school to his grandparents' house, which was only three blocks away from his own. He remembers his grandparents taking great care of him and Jimmy. He also remembers the influence of his English heritage, from the four o'clock tea time to the room-temperature soda. The only thing they kept chilled was milk—for John. Dinners came late in the afternoon. John soaked it all in, from the British sense of humor to the vocabulary to the emphasis on certain words.

All the while John's mother's side of the family, from the Azores, a group of small islands west of Portugal in the mid-Atlantic, was also a constant presence in his life. His mom and her siblings had grown up in a shared household with the Perez family. The families remained connected, so much so that John thought he was part of the Perez family until he was thirteen. He was not happy when he found out they were not blood relatives. They all helped each other, working in the factories in the south end of their city, sharing their immigrant upbringing and the promise of a better life in America.

Growing up, John knew without a doubt that he wanted to be either a priest or a teacher. His high school years were typical; he played sports, including football, and showed an aptitude for literature. It appeared the priesthood was going to win young John's career affections, but then he discovered girls. So teaching became his profession, and he never really veered from that path.

At the young age of twenty-four, after graduating from Bridgewater State College, John received a teaching contract from New Bedford High School. He made lots of friends through teaching, many of whom are still his closest friends today. Together they basked in the glow of impacting young minds while also becoming a support system for one another. Six years into his teaching profession, it appeared that his career path was set. But then a long relationship ended, and suddenly he found himself with no strings and some savings in his pocket. There was no longer anything to keep him in New Bedford, and so along with a group of friends, he set out for California.

But something had been gnawing at John. He believed he was missing something in the world of teaching; he felt constrained and unable to expand his horizons. What's more, he was afraid he would become staid and domestic, a rubber stamp with no point to his existence, simply passing time mirroring the social line of doing what one was supposed to do, dressing as one was supposed to dress, and speaking as one was supposed to speak. California—warm, adventurous, and on the opposite side of the country—presented an opportunity to break away from those constraints, to *become* a character rather than a teacher of them. And the pages he would fill with adventures would be his own life story and not that of someone else.

The West Coast did not disappoint. John found adrenaline, excitement, surprise, and a way of life that was completely different from the East Coast. No two days were the same.

He spent most of the time working as a ski instructor and a snowmaker at a ski resort not far from San Bernardino. He enjoyed teaching skiing plenty but snowmaking not as much, in part because it isn't nearly as glamorous as it sounds. The machines have to be watched throughout the night and readjusted as the temperature drops. This same process unfolds during the day as well. One morning while working high up on a hill making snow, John caught a glimpse of a school bus down in the valley below. From that height, he watched the yellow bus wind its way through the community, children climbing eagerly onto the school bus, their parents lingering curbside. That was the world John had left, and he realized in that moment that he longed for it still. He had found adventure in California, but life had lost its meaning, and he would not find it making snow on a hill. Transforming young minds was what he was meant to do. When ski season came to a close in April, he headed home determined to return to teaching.

When John was back in Massachusetts, a friend mentioned he might fit in the Upward Bound program. John thought the program might give him a more flexible schedule, though he would be giving up earning power. But this was a concession he was willing to make. He had what he needed—freedom and flexibility. He'd also left behind his small cottage when he ventured west but much to his delight was able to rent it back.

John had left Massachusetts to be his own character, but in the summer of '79, he met a whole new set of characters in the Upward Bound program. They were writing their own life novels, and every one of them was an interesting read. John found he couldn't put the book down. Teaching and counseling these young people provided far greater stories than any he could get from a book—and what's more, he could help them write their chapters.

The students in the program presented a sharp contrast to the way John had grown up. His heart went out to them, for many of them dealt with challenging circumstances. He knew he didn't have the perfect advice for all of them. What he did know was he could help them along by traveling with them on their life journeys, something like an older scout guiding a younger one. He could stand in the background and whisper soft advice: "Hey, I tried it that way, it didn't work out well for me. Try it this way. But I'm going to support you no matter what decision you make."

Four years later John was still living a singular existence in his cottage a short ride from the beach. He had what he needed, with no worries for the immediate future. He had a job and was living life day-to-day, making enough money to pay his bills. Still a bachelor, he existed happily on the line of existence and subsistence. But a familiar yearning to do more with his life had resurfaced.

Upward Bound was a federal program administered by a state college (University of Massachusetts Dartmouth), and John was part of a small group of teachers that would support the program through additional instruction. Since the program was accessed through local universities, the Upward Bound offices were required to be open during winter break when high schools were closed. This requirement held true on that cold December day. Since John wasn't married and didn't have children, he was the one who manned the office during Christmas break. He would get New Year's Eve off.

It was four o'clock in the afternoon when Mike Silvia called. There had been virtually no calls that day. John didn't know at the time that I had been in Mike's office for most of the day, desperately looking for a miracle. Mike had perfected his plea by this time, but he knew John was my last hope. He spoke quickly and more urgently: "One of our clients needs an emergency removal from a foster home. We are having trouble placing him . . . it would only be a temporary stay . . . because it's Christmastime, I can't get ahold of anyone." He rambled on, "Do you know anyone who might be able to take him . . . temporarily?"

John was quiet, trying to process all he'd just heard. "John, his name is Steve Klakowicz," Mike said, referring to my birth name. "Do you think you can take him until the start of the new year?"

John answered right away, with no hesitation, "Yes, absolutely."

His response changed my life.

I had found myself in the midst of a storm that was not of my creation, uncertain of the direction my journey would take me. But then suddenly, in the midst of that storm, when all seemed lost, a lighthouse appeared. What I did not know then, and did not fully realize until sometime later, was that John was in the middle of his own storm, desperately trying to find his own lighthouse.

The lighthouse effect is the idea that ordinary people, immersed in the business of their own lives, wrestling with their own struggles and imperfections, can touch the lives of others. It suggests that our lives are formed, altered, and characterized by the smallest of interactions that bend the arc of our lives. It means that we see our life experience as an opportunity to touch the life of another, to see in their life a connection to our own. It is a framework for living, learning, and leading, a way to more positively engage with one another, to build trust, to see beyond the labels that define us to the human experiences that bond us.

We all have the capacity to be a lighthouse. You may think you have to be famous, wealthy, or gifted with a once-in-a-lifetime talent to be a lighthouse. You may think you need advanced degrees or special certification. You may be of the opinion that you aren't accomplished enough or don't have a big enough title to be that shining light. Or that you simply don't have the time.

> **Your life experience is an opportunity to touch the life of another, to see in their life a connection to your own.**

You'd be wrong. Everything you need to be a lighthouse you already have—your own journey, your own seemingly ordinary story, even with all its imperfections. That brings me to the first effect of the lighthouse: turning doubts into destinations.

The Lighthouse Effect: Turning Doubts into Destinations

John understood that years of ridicule and constant criticism from the foster family had taken a toll on my self-confidence. *Dumb. Ugly. Something about you is not right.* Where there should have been optimism and idealism, there was nothing but uncertainty and skepticism. Watching my social worker desperately try to find me a place to stay had only furthered those emotions.

We've all had them or faced them—doubts about our value and our place in the world, worries that we are not enough or haven't done enough. Perhaps it is something that was said to us or a project that did not work out the way we planned. Doubt paralyzes us into complacency and then fools us into believing that safety is found in doing nothing at all. Doubt has an accomplice: fear—fear of being rejected, fear of failing, or fear of disappointing. It thrives most on comparison, especially in the world of social media, where in a universe of edited existences and flawless filters, many lives appear to be perfect. Doubts can become a living, breathing entity that suffocates every dream we've ever had. It can hold us hostage. But we can erase those doubts for ourselves, and we can help others do the same. We can turn doubts into destinations.

Doubt is largely a lack of confidence in a direction, a decision, or a person. It means we aren't entirely sure of an outcome. When we unpack doubt a bit more, we realize that doubt is fear brought on by a lack of information, experience, or preparation. It can also come from a prior setback or bad experience. To be fair, some doubt is quite beneficial, a cautious skepticism that helps us make more informed decisions. The doubt I am describing here is not healthy doubt but the paralyzing kind that freezes us in our tracks. To turn your doubts into destinations, try some of the following tips.

Remember a Time When You Were at Your Best

Think of a time when you were at your best. It might have been a presentation you delivered, a home project that went flawlessly, or a work plan that you led successfully. Do you recall the compliments and notes of congratulations for a job well done? Do you remember how that made you feel, knowing that your effort had been recognized? It's possible you were just having a good day, but it's more likely that you prepared differently for that situation. You looked at every detail, anticipated challenges, and had a backup plan if something did not go as expected. In other words, your success in that moment was no accident. Your confidence in the outcome came because your preparation, execution, and knowledge all lined up perfectly.

We have become adept at analyzing setbacks to the point of exhaustion. We don't spend nearly as much time examining our successes, in part because we believe it might lead to complacency or a false sense of security. But by understanding what we did well, we create a blueprint, a foundation of strength on which future successes are built—a resilient place where future doubts will be unable to take hold. Remember we're talking about *your* best, not someone else's. I have found a line from Max Ehrmann's poem "Desiderata" quite helpful:

> If you compare yourself with others
> you may become vain or bitter;
> for always there will be greater or lesser persons than
> yourself.

When you use comparison to define your best, you open the door wide open for doubt to walk in and wreak havoc on your life.

Take Risks and Encourage Others to Do the Same

"Nothing ventured, nothing gained" goes the old saying, and this timeless, simple mantra has remained consistently true. There is no such thing as failure, because even when a setback occurs, a lesson is learned. This was John's lighthouse effect; though he knew I would be denied some scholarship offers, I would learn a greater lesson on the importance of advocating for oneself and being willing to take risks to do so. There is always something to be gained from taking a risk, whether it is a successful outcome or we adjust our course because of what we learned.

Say Yes

As the years pass, my gratitude and appreciation for what John did have only deepened. He was going about his daily life and then put that life on hold to provide me a home. One time I asked him what he was thinking the day my social worker called him. Here is what he said:

> It was a shock, I can tell you that. Initially, I was just trying to understand what he was saying and who he was talking about. When I realized it was you he was talking about and that he was really asking if you could stay with me, I had a lingering moment of doubt. Not about you, because I knew you and I loved you already; the doubt was more about me. Teaching teenagers was one thing but bringing one into my home was another. As your social worker was talking to me, I was talking to God. "God," I said, "I don't know if I'm good enough to do this." I guess it was an

on-the-spot prayer, and what God said back to me was, "This young man is out of options and he needs you. So I'm going to need you to trust me. I need you to say yes." And I did. From that day to this day, I never regretted it.

The opportunity to say yes appears often over the course of our lives. Sometimes it comes in the form of a quiet whisper or a silent plea. Like John, you may have your doubts as to whether you are capable, have the time, or possess the skills to help. The timing might not feel right. When you say yes, even if it is to something small, you can affect the life of another in ways you can never imagine.

Find the Source of Your Doubts

Doubt is often a quiet story we tell ourselves about why something can't be achieved. But it has a source, a reason why it exists. To overcome doubt, we need to determine its origins. Did your doubt stem from an opinion or a criticism? A message from childhood that you've held on to? A time when a setback was broadcast publicly? A private struggle?

Whatever the experience, admitting that we harbor such feelings can be difficult. We are afraid to show our vulnerability or are uncertain where to turn for solutions. Suffering in silence, struggling to find a way forward, we find ourselves locked in a perpetual cycle of uncertainty. This was the place John found himself when he, who had been a lighthouse to so many others, needed one of his own.

My favorite photo of John Sykes is almost thirty years old. Hurricane Bob, one of the costliest hurricanes in New England history, barreled up the East Coast, landing in Massachusetts with destructive gale force winds. That afternoon John and a group of friends decided they would ride out the storm by gathering together at the Mattapoisett Inn, a local pub just a stone's throw from the Atlantic Ocean. Suddenly there was a commotion. A group of people went sprinting past the pub's windows, and John and his friends went out to join them, not certain where the group was going but suspecting that someone needed help. They were right; a novice sailor was desperately trying to get their boat out of the water before the hurricane arrived. He had underestimated the ferocity of the hurricane winds, and the boat had slid off the trailer and dangled precariously over the precipice of the landing dock, threatening to tip over on its side into the ocean.

John and a group of men grabbed the boat, courageously trying to pull it onto the dock. If it fell over, it would be swept out to sea. A photographer, documenting the storm's impact in the region, snapped a picture of the men. In the photo you can see John stretching and straining against the wind and the weight of the boat. His hair is a wet mop, and his face, usually calm and placid, is contorted and twisted as he uses every bit of strength to bring the boat back onto the dock. It appears as if he is taking on a great battle, and he was. But it wasn't just against the storm. He was also wrestling against a different kind of beast just as merciless and destructive. Unlike the storm, this battle had no end in sight: John was battling alcoholism.

It was a problem that had begun quietly in college, and while he believed he had control over his drinking, the passing years held a different truth. John did not have control over alcohol; it had control over him.

During the year and a half I lived with John before heading off to college, I sensed that he was struggling with alcohol. He wasn't mean or angry when he drank, nor did he ever allow it to interfere with his teaching. Still, he drank to the point where I quietly wondered if he had a bigger problem. I was too young to know how to help, and at that phase in his battle, he would not have listened to me—or anyone else. While I was in college, his drinking had apparently become a much greater problem, driven by a loneliness that he couldn't understand or overcome. One day a group of his closest friends knocked on his door and told him they needed to talk. At that point John, who had hit rock bottom, was finally willing to listen to their advice to get the help he needed.

As he went through his recovery process, he saw that part of the reason he turned toward alcohol was because of loneliness and self-doubt. Those who know him, both his friends and students, know what he means to them. But John wasn't able to see that for himself. Still, he fully committed himself to recovery, and twenty-five-years later, he has remained sober. No one ever declares victory over alcoholism, and so it is something he continues to work on every day.

The most difficult examinations are the ones that require us to take a hard look at ourselves and confront the things we don't like. John's willingness to face the disease of alcoholism, to no longer allow it to hold him hostage, was a lighthouse moment for John. He has been a tireless advocate for and supporter of Alcoholics Anonymous and is often a resource for those who are still trying to find their own path to recovery. Many years after taking a last-chance call about a desperate teenager, John Sykes remains a lighthouse.

John and I still talk the way we did when I first lived with him. We talk about my children, world events, and over the years something that neither of us has been able to fully explain: the extraordinary circumstances that brought us together. One particular time our conversation turned to our favorite books again, something we had not discussed since we once sat together at the small kitchen table in his one-bedroom cottage.

"Something just occurred to me," he said one evening. "I better understand now why *Of Mice and Men* is my favorite book. It's a story about needing someone to love and someone needing to be loved. That story is also *our* story."

CHAPTER 2

RJ

*Love is the most important thing in the
world, but baseball is pretty good too.*
—YOGI BERRA

Baseball was America's first sports love. And though more recently other sports have surged in popularity, baseball still has a particular place in America. It is the nation's oldest pastime, beating out football by twenty-three years. Baseball begins in the spring, the season of new beginnings, and each fall, as the leaves descend and coolness fills the air, the game departs, heading to its winter rest. In between, the sounds of baseball often fill our neighborhoods: the crack (or the ping) of the bat, the popping sound of the ball arriving in a glove, or the crunching of cleats on the ground as a runner sprints for home plate.

Baseball is a sport that is passed down from generation

to generation, and it is also deeply intertwined with our own national story. It helped pave the way for the end of segregation in America and also helped us come together after the tragic events of 9/11. Allegiances to our hometown baseball teams run deep. Growing up in New England, or Red Sox Nation as it is commonly referenced, I have long mused that you're more likely to meet a unicorn than to meet a former Red Sox fan. Rooting for the Red Sox—and against their archrival, the Yankees—is a lifelong habit. But even among these loyal fandoms, the reverence for the game reigns supreme. Because of that reverence, baseball fans have an appreciation for teams other than their own, and one of those teams is the Los Angeles Dodgers.

Initially founded in Brooklyn in 1883, the Dodgers moved to Los Angeles in 1958. But it was while they were in Brooklyn that the Dodgers would make arguably their most important contribution to baseball when they signed Jackie Robinson, making him the first African American to play in the big leagues. When the team moved west, the story of Jackie Robinson stayed with the franchise, and all of baseball. In April 1997, Major League Baseball announced that No. 42, Robinson's number with the Brooklyn Dodgers, would be permanently retired throughout the sport.

A Major League Baseball clubhouse is a finely tuned machine. It has to be because it is made of a hundred moving parts that must be highly coordinated. This responsibility falls to the clubhouse staff whose assignments run the gamut of getting uniforms ready to preparing the postgame meal to running errands for the players. Their day begins before the sun rises and ends long after it has set. When game day arrives, the clubhouse, which is the pulse of the team, becomes a beehive of activity.

At the center of the action in the Los Angeles Dodgers clubhouse is a tall, slender, and undeniably handsome twenty-three-year-old man, known to all as RJ. When he enters the clubhouse, the energy suddenly changes among his fellow clubhouse attendants and the Dodgers players. The steady sound of man-hugs and backslaps fills the room. RJ loves being in the clubhouse, as if there is no other place he would rather be. Everyone knows this and they feed off his spirit. The baseball season is a long grind, and RJ's sunny optimism is exactly the kind of energy that is needed to get through it. It is hard to have a bad day when he is near.

He brings more than good-natured disposition to the Dodgers clubhouse. RJ is really good at his job. He is punctual and thrives on routine. He is relentless about detail, whether that be folding towels or hanging the players' uniforms in their locker stalls just so. He does everything with precision and accuracy and follows through on any task he is assigned. "RJ has it handled" is a common phrase heard in the Dodgers clubhouse.

You would never know this is RJ's first job. Nor would you know it was once predicted that RJ would never find a meaningful livelihood.

Until the age of two, RJ met every childhood milestone. But that all came to a halt when he suddenly stopped connecting and communicating. He stopped making eye contact, interacting with his mother, and playing with his twin sister. Though RJ's mom and dad were first-time parents, they still knew the children should have the same pace of progress: they should walk and talk around the same time. When RJ's development lagged behind his sister's, his parents expressed their concern to the pediatrician. "Nothing is wrong with RJ. He's a boy and we know they develop a little bit slower than girls." They both breathed a sigh of relief.

But as the months unfolded, RJ's development not only stopped but began to regress. Now he had gone silent. More visits to the doctor led to a similar conclusion: RJ is just maturing a little later. While his dad accepted this assessment, his mom was less convinced. Her mommy radar kept telling her that something wasn't quite right, that the well-intentioned doctor was missing something. For over a year, they tried to understand what was happening with RJ.

As RJ's childhood development continued to lag, the family sought additional opinions, and those opinions confirmed what his mother had already begun to suspect: RJ had autism. The diagnosis was a staggering blow, stinging all the more because it was delivered with a cold prediction: "RJ is definitely on the autism spectrum. That means he will never say 'I love you.' He will never play team sports. He will never look you in the eye or have a meaningful conversation with you." His mom burst into tears, and his dad, while trying to be stoic, was quietly devastated.

When we learn our child is coming into the world, we envision what that child will be like. We imagine their personality, their first words, and their first steps. We imagine them jumping into our arms and reading bedtime stories together. We think of them skinning their knee and the bandages and small kisses that will make it all better. We forecast their future too, imagining them as young adults, coming of age and trying to find their place in the world as we once did. We wish for them a life of safety and good health, one also filled with opportunity and normalcy. But a diagnosis of autism shatters those dreams, and the beautiful future you once imagined is different now, brimming with a thousand questions you can't get the answers to. Adding to that are the emotions of panic, anxiety, sadness, and a nagging feeling that you've done something wrong.

This is the cycle of emotions that RJ's parents went through. For them, there was another layer of emotions. His dad is Rodney Peete, the famed USC quarterback who finished second in the Heisman voting and had a sixteen-year NFL career; his mom is Holly Robinson Peete, the renowned actress and singer known for her roles on some of America's most popular sitcoms.

On paper their life was idyllic. Their marriage, their wedding, and their family were so beautiful. On the evening of their wedding, Rodney signed with Holly's hometown Eagles, the team she and her dad had rooted for. During Rodney's second season in Philadelphia, they learned they were pregnant, with twins no less. They were suddenly like the First Family of Philadelphia—the star quarterback and the famous actress. On the day the twins were delivered, the cover of the *Philadelphia Daily News* showcased Rodney, with a picture of him running away from all the Arizona Cardinal defenders and a headline that read "Rodney Peete—OT-GYN." The game had gone to overtime, and Rodney needed a waiting police escort to bring him to the hospital so that he could witness the arrival of the twins. He led his team to victory and, legend has it, kept going right to the police car. He would arrive just in the nick of time.

The Peetes' life and marriage were the stories of which fairy tales are made, and nowhere in those tales is there a chapter about having a child diagnosed with autism. It would take some time for the new reality to sink in. Both Holly and Rodney struggled to grasp RJ's inability to process the world. There was no instruction manual to follow, no signs pointing the way toward healing—for RJ or for them. Shortly after the diagnosis, the family had been vacationing in Martha's Vineyard when RJ wandered into the path of a fast-moving vehicle. Only Holly's bloodcurdling scream averted a tragedy. But RJ's inability to understand the seriousness of the near-catastrophe was a further reminder of how much their life had changed. Their hopes and dreams of a normal childhood had been replaced with a different reality.

For Rodney, that reality was hard to accept. An outstanding college athlete who excelled in two sports, he had found athletic success by imposing his will. He thought autism would be no different. It was an opponent to be defeated as any other opponent had to be. There was something else too. He'd had fond memories of early childhood years with his own dad, playing catch and learning about life. He wanted RJ, who bore his name, to have those same memories. He wanted RJ to be his little man, to join him in the locker room after games. And he imagined sitting in the audience as a proud dad when it was announced his son had won the Heisman Trophy. But autism had stolen those memories before they could even be made and had done so without giving him a say in the matter.

By his own admission, this new world was a real struggle for Rodney. He thought he could coach autism out of RJ and they could get back to building their father-son bond. When that strategy failed, Rodney quietly withdrew as the strain of RJ's diagnosis began to take a toll on the family.

Meanwhile, Holly was having her own struggles. Throughout RJ's diagnosis and early childhood, Holly had heard the "never" prediction over and over again. Though she advocated otherwise, she had quietly begun to buy into this theory—that the RJ she saw now was the one she would always see. Her response to this was to smother her son, to try to protect him from getting hurt or embarrassed or misunderstood.

For Rodney it all changed the day he got on the floor and immersed himself in RJ's world rather than try to pull him out of it. And suddenly it clicked: he didn't need to raise RJ to be a better version of him but rather to help RJ be the best version of RJ. Holly had a similar breakthrough when RJ attended his first event without her. He did so only because Holly's mom, Dolores, had insisted. "It's time you stop hanging over him," she had told her daughter. And RJ not only did fine but excelled without Holly's presence.

In their own way, each parent had come to the same realization: autism could be neither willed nor hugged away. It was an understanding that brought them closer together, saved their marriage, and provided RJ the kind of support he needed.

One in fifty-four children are diagnosed with autism every year.[1] Of these, 40 percent are defined as nonverbal.[2] Parents of a child with autism struggle with the fears of what the child will not be. Though they understand that being on the autism spectrum is variable and that those with autism can still have meaningful lives, the dread of what might not be still looms. They may not make friends. They may not go to college. They may never obtain a driver's license. They may never be independent. They may never marry or raise a family. They may never have a job. And another thought always haunts parents of children with autism or any other disability: What will happen to them if something happens to me?

The answer to these questions for the Peete family was to lean into RJ's diagnosis with the kind of intensity that defined their family. While providing RJ the support he needed, the family became tireless advocates for raising awareness of autism. The HollyRod Foundation (www .hollyrod.org) was initially founded to support the cause of Parkinson's, which had afflicted Holly's dad, Matt Robinson. Now it was expanded to include autism. HollyRod launched the RJ's Place grant to provide assistive technology to children's hospitals and autism centers. As children with autism get older, they require vocational training and specialized job placement assistance to transition to mainstream life and gainful employment. This grant now supports toddlers to young adults in over a dozen locations across the US and Canada.

The impact of the foundation has been far-reaching, in part because of the Peete family's willingness to share their autism journey, from denial and surrender to embrace and ambassadorship. The Peetes had decided that RJ's journey could be helpful to other families struggling with the same.

In 2010 Rodney published a book about his father-son journey, titled *Not My Boy*, which features a beaming RJ and Rodney on the front cover.

Holly has been a particular force behind the foundation. "I wouldn't change RJ for the world, but I would change the world for RJ," she once thought. And she has set about doing exactly that. From the outset she poured herself into learning everything she could about autism and its impact. That has primarily shown up in the way she talks about the HollyRod Foundation because she does so with such passion and authenticity that you can't help but be swept up in the cause. Yet at the forefront of that passion has always been a mother's love for her son—and a desire to raise awareness.

One evening in May a few years ago, I attended a charity event in downtown Chicago. Holly and RJ flew from Los Angeles, and Holly was to be honored at this major black-tie gala for her many contributions to autism awareness. She dressed in a resplendent emerald-green dress, and he was neatly attired in a light-gray pinstripe suit and open-collared white shirt. They walked the event's red carpet, greeting guests and mingling with the other honorees. Later in the evening, Holly and RJ approached the podium. In a moment that could never have been imagined, RJ, of whom it was predicted would never be able to have a meaningful conversation, was going to introduce his mother to hundreds of people in a sold-out ballroom. It would be the biggest speech he'd ever given.

Public speaking is a great fear for many people; this is especially true for those on the autism spectrum. Processing new information happens a bit more slowly, and this can make speaking from a script particularly challenging. When those with autism present, their speech can become halting as they search for the right words. They are aware of this, of course, and become nervous as a result. The answer to this dilemma is to memorize every single word of the script. This plays into one of the many strengths that people with autism have; their long-term memory and particular ability to recall facts are truly extraordinary. This is why RJ and his mom had prepared his remarks weeks in advance and had gone over them several times in their hotel room right before the event.

RJ walked up to the podium, grabbed the end of it with outstretched arms, and then did something they had not planned: he went off script. Holly, standing slightly behind RJ, tensed, ready to intervene if he began to struggle. But it became clear that RJ was not only in complete command of the stage and the audience but had in fact planned this diversion without telling his mother.

Soon it became clear why.

First, I want to thank my family for always loving and protecting me. It has been a long, difficult journey with autism. In the sixth grade I wrote a poem called "Yesterday and Today." It started: "Yesterday I could not speak, and today I can't stop talking." I remember that everyone clapped. I still have my struggles, but I am so happy to be able to finally tell the world how I feel. When I couldn't talk, I could still understand what people said about me. Always remember that. I want all kids with autism to know how amazing they are.[3]

There was an uncommon silence in the room. No tinkling of glasses or rattling of silverware could be heard as RJ spoke. Finally, he directed his comments to his mom:

I just want you to know I am so glad you are my mom. You say a lot that you are proud of me, but I am the one who is proud of you. I love you, Mom.

The room didn't jump to its feet as much it exploded. Many of us were in tears or close to it. As the applause went on, I made eye contact with Dwyane Wade, the NBA legend who was also being honored that night, and we both shook our heads in mutual amazement. Like many in the room, we'd heard a lot of speeches but never anything quite like that.

Watching the room embrace her son, Holly had a flashback to years earlier, that initial devastating diagnosis and the prediction about what RJ would not do. She remembered, too, the struggles in her marriage as they tried to come to terms with his diagnosis. She remembered the many odd stares sent in their direction as RJ's autism manifested itself in public and the awkward moments when well-intentioned people would apologize for his "disease." Yet here RJ was, defying every limitation that had ever been placed on him.

"He is finding his voice," she thought. The emotion of the moment overwhelmed her as she put her hands to her face and blinked back tears of joy and gratitude.

While RJ continued to exceed expectations, there was one wall that he had not managed to climb: employment. He had graduated from high school but had struggled to find a meaningful job that would keep him engaged. This is common for people with disabilities—they are twice as likely to be unemployed, compared with those without a disability.[4] Often they are caught in a quandary as to whether they should disclose that they have a disability; they worry that there is still a stigma attached and that employers will no longer show an interest if they volunteer this information.

Employment for people with disabilities is about more than having a job; it is also a pathway to achieving independence. For some, it means being able to make their own decisions and to have some control over their life. For others, it allows them to be a contributor to society and to connect socially. I saw this firsthand during my time as a corporate executive at Walgreens. The company was a pioneer in employing people with disabilities, and on more than one occasion, I witnessed an individual who had existed on the periphery of employment receive their very first paycheck. I could see the joy and elation so beautifully imprinted on their faces. I could see what it meant to their parents, who now could envision a path to self-sufficiency for their child. This was the future that Holly and Rodney wanted for RJ, but it was proving to be elusive.

Then help came from a most unlikely place. In finding

his voice, RJ was also *becoming* a voice for those with autism. He was often featured in articles or stories, especially during April, recognized across the world as National Autism Awareness Month. During one particular interview, RJ talked about his desire to find employment. Watching that interview, unbeknownst to the family, was Lon Rosen, the LA Dodgers executive vice president and chief marketing officer. He called Magic Johnson, the basketball legend and also co-owner of the Los Angeles Dodgers, and the two men discussed the possibility of employing RJ. Magic was more than receptive to the idea; he had known RJ his entire life. Lon immediately called Holly and told her the Dodgers might have a position for RJ and invited him to come in for an interview. Not surprisingly, RJ impressed everyone he met, from Dodgers manager Dave Roberts to players like Clayton Kershaw and Justin Turner. Shortly thereafter, RJ was hired to serve as one of their new clubhouse attendants.

Over the years, Holly had purposefully built a network of support around RJ. She knew that while RJ was surrounded by support at home with family and friends, he also needed to develop a sense of community in the outside world. So was born "team RJ," a village of individuals who are wrapped around RJ and who are available at a moment's notice. They are people like Dr. Pam Wiley, RJ's therapist who gave him the gift of language, and Lon Rosen, who has become his "work dad." But when you talk to team RJ and ask them about their commitment to him, it becomes clear that RJ has had an extraordinary impact on them and many others.

When he was fourteen years old, RJ became a camp counselor for younger kids with autism. Ranging in ages from toddlers to five years old, the children sometimes struggled in the camp setting.

One day, when Holly arrived to collect RJ, a parent approached and asked, "Are you RJ's mom?"

"Yes, I am," she replied pleasantly.

The man continued, "Today RJ walked up to me when I came to pick up my son, and he said, 'I really enjoyed being with your son today.'" The man paused as tears welled in his eyes. "Nobody has ever said that about my son, that they enjoyed being around him or that they liked talking or interacting with him."

On the way home, Holly recounted the conversation for RJ: "RJ, when parents send their kids with autism to school or camp, especially when they are younger, we are worried about whether someone is going to do something to them when they can't talk or defend themselves. We also worry that people don't want to be around them. What you said made that dad feel so good. Why did you say that?" she asked.

RJ shrugged. "I just wanted him to know that his son was really nice."

As RJ has gotten older, he has made younger people with autism his priority. When Holly tells RJ that he is going to meet a young person with autism, one of his first questions is: "Can he talk?" When he is around others with autism, he transforms. His energy shifts and he squints his eyes, peering at his new friend as if he is reading them. He always asks their counselors or teachers about their capabilities, trying to make any kind of connection with them. And they respond and interact with him, as if they have a special language the rest of us aren't privy to.

The Lighthouse Effect:
Possibilities over Circumstances

Wherever you see a lighthouse, the sound of a pounding surf is always nearby. At Wind Point Lighthouse in Wisconsin, the roar of Lake Michigan is just a few yards away, welcoming visitors with unapologetic ferocity. Wave after wave punishes the enormous boulders that have been placed there to form a seawall. It is then that you begin to get a sense of the power of the waves, their relentless force smashing into the rocks, mocking their attempt to stop them, as if they know that the stones will eventually wear down. You begin to see what the lighthouse is up against, the endless swells that will not compromise or negotiate. In that world, all you can see are circumstances.

When RJ and his family were presented with his autism diagnosis, it was the equivalent of those pounding waves, presenting them with conditions that seemed fixed and binding. This same scenario happens in many of our daily lives, circumstances that aren't of our making presenting us with challenges for which we are not prepared. They can be as small as car trouble or far more significant, such as the loss of a job.

Get above the Circumstance

One of the ways the lighthouse defies the storm is with one of its defining features: its dazzling height, stretching upward as if a circular beanstalk reaching into the clouds. From this height, the lighthouse allows us to see the surroundings more clearly and visibly. Those circumstances that from ground level seemed impossible to navigate now look a bit different. We can see the break in the waves that from the shore seemed so relentless. Suddenly, we can see our way around the reefs and the rocks and the prior shipwrecks that doomed other sailors. We can make new mistakes and not old ones. From this height, the circumstances need no longer define us or control our journey. We no longer make excuses or place the blame on others. We are able to understand the situation and try to navigate it as best we can. Though we are still aware of the circumstances, our focus is now entirely on the possibilities.

The Power of the Pivot

A different vantage point gives us new information, and with that information we can begin to change our approach. You can see this quite clearly in the way Rodney and Holly pivoted from RJ's life-altering diagnosis to creating the different ways in which he could connect and thrive. When Rodney immersed himself in RJ's world, he saw autism from a different perspective. When Holly saw RJ excel without her by his side, she then saw a brighter future for him. They arrived at this realization in different ways and at different times, but in each instance they did the same thing: pivoting from the circumstance to the possibility. This skill is one of several attributes our human lighthouses have in common.

Pivoting does not mean changing your goal but rather changing your strategy to realize that goal. Successful people often pivot at some point in their lives; many will do so multiple times and across multiple dimensions of their life, from their relationships and friendships to their career decisions and the way they spend their money. This approach accepts that situations do change and that the strategies we used in one instance no longer apply.

There is an important aspect of pivoting: time. How long does it take us to make that pivot? Early on in my professional career, I felt stuck. I had been in a career I enjoyed, but my opportunities to grow and progress were limited. Not knowing exactly what to do next or how, I remained in that role five years longer than I should have. It was an important career lesson and one that I have remembered ever since: don't take too long to pivot. It's not always easy. We go through a process of ignoring the whispers in our own heart. What forced me to pivot in my professional career was a wonderful call from my wife, Tonya, telling me that we were expecting our first child. I remember the sheer joy of that news—"I'm going to be a Dad!" I also knew we were not making enough money to raise a family. Another urgent thought hit me: "You have to get moving."

> Pivoting does not mean changing your goal but rather changing your strategy to realize that goal.

Independent of life-changing news, knowing when to pivot can be a challenge. While it can be different depending on the circumstance, there are often telltale signs. You wake up every day feeling as if you are stuck. You have to dig deep to get through a day. You don't feel as if you are growing or learning. You find yourself easily distracted or indulging in procrastinating behaviors like binge-watching shows or doomscrolling on social media. Your patience level is not particularly high. When Sunday evening rolls around, you sigh heavily at the prospect of returning to another week of routine that you don't like.

Purposeful Planning

Purposeful planning is an essential part of moving from circumstances to possibilities. A good place to begin is by gauging where you stand across the dimensions of your life. A popular practice I have found to be effective is "stop, start, continue." You get a piece of paper, and at the top of the page you create three separate columns. You label those columns "stop," "start," "continue." What do you want to stop doing? This requires you to look backward and have an honest conversation with yourself about things you want to change. What—and sometimes who—is getting in the way of reaching the possibility you now see?

Stop	Start	Continue

Stopping in and of itself is not enough, and if that is all you focus on, then you run the risk of becoming overly self-critical and inadequate. What do you want to start doing? These items are always positive and require you *to do something,* to become engaged in a behavior that gets you closer to your goal. Otherwise, you are just hoping, and hoping leaves decisions and directions in other people's hands.

Stopping and starting go hand in hand. For example, you can certainly acknowledge that you want to stop spending so much time on social media, but that is more likely to happen if you start exercising more. In his influential book *The Power of Habit*, Charles Duhigg noted, "To change a habit, you must keep the old cue, and deliver the old reward, but insert a new routine."[5] At first glance, the start phase of this process can seem large and daunting. But breaking down the effort and taking small steps toward the goal can be an effective strategy in overcoming anxiety about the size of the task you are taking on.

The things you want to continue allow you to look at the aspects of your life that you feel are working effectively. Those can also be activities that bring you joy or sanctuary. Considering activities you want to continue also performs another important function: it allows you to acknowledge and celebrate your strong suits as well as your capabilities. In this framework, "Continue" is no less important than "stop" and "start." It reminds you of your value and your contributions—to your family, your organization, and your community.

Purposeful planning is most effective when you are actively seeking and getting feedback from those whose judgment you trust and respect. Remember Dolores Robinson's advice to her daughter? "I know how much you love RJ, and he will always need your love and support. But now you have to stop smothering him. Start giving him room to grow and find his own voice." What Holly's mom did in that moment was provide helpful feedback to her daughter and did so in a way that wasn't focused only on what she should stop doing but rather on what she could start doing. At the same time, she acknowledged the things that Holly needed to continue doing.

Personal Accountability

The last component of moving from circumstances to possibilities is about our responsibility to ourselves. That's what accountability really is—fulfilling a promise to ourselves. Without it, achieving a new direction is virtually impossible. When we hold ourselves accountable, we also remind ourselves of our talents and capabilities. Place your "stop, start, continue" framework somewhere you can see it regularly. Use to-do lists to measure your progress. Find a buddy who will join you on your accountability journey. Most important of all, be honest with yourself. Don't let excuses or procrastination hold you hostage.

While in college, I pledged a fraternity that has a long history of developing leaders in every field of human endeavor. Part of the reason for this successful blueprint was an emphasis on personal accountability. This was best reflected in a mantra the older brothers made all new members memorize: *Excuses are tools of the incompetent reserved to build monuments to nothing, and those who dwell in them are seldom good for anything else.*

One sunny spring morning, a sea of familiar Dodger blue takes to a baseball diamond in Southern California. But it is not for a baseball game. Rather, they are there to break ground on the latest Dodgers Dreamfield. Several years ago the franchise committed to building baseball diamonds in and around the Los Angeles area that would serve as places for young people to enjoy the game.

This field will be different. It is a universally accessible field designed for youth with special needs and physical disabilities, serving the three thousand youth with special needs in the surrounding neighborhood. It looks like a smaller version of Dodger Stadium, from the rubber surfaces, enlarged dugouts, and player benches to the outfield signage. The Dodgers, who once showed America what an equal and accessible world can look like and how much better we are for it, are now adding another chapter to that story.

A few days earlier, RJ had stood proudly on the first base line at Dodger Stadium as he was introduced along with coaches and players on opening day. Here he was again, celebrating the opening of a baseball diamond that was meant for young people just like him, demonstrating once again the power of possibility. After the ceremony he would head right to Dodger Stadium to resume his duties as clubhouse attendant. Later that night, the Dodgers would take to the field against their long-standing rival the San Francisco Giants and defeat them in a thrilling game that went down to the last out.[6]

RJ does not fully comprehend the effect he has on the world. He doesn't understand why many of his idols insist on seeing him whenever they come to a Dodgers game. Nor is he aware of why young children with autism flock to him.

He can't grasp the magnitude of the admiration that many people have for him and the times his parents silently stare in awe at the young man he continues to become.

Yet there are times you can see him out on the baseball diamond, staring off into the beautifully lit Southern California sky, leaning forward, elbows resting on his knees, chewing gum like the Big Leaguers do, proudly wearing his Dodger blue. In his expressive brown eyes, he appears to be taking it all in, a mixture of quiet gratitude and peaceful reflection. In that moment, RJ Peete, the young boy whose early years were defined by what he would not do, stands amid so much history, contributing his own chapter to the timeless story of the power of possibility.

CHAPTER 3

FL KIRBY

*I have fought the good fight, I have
finished the race, I have kept the faith.*
—2 TIMOTHY 4:7

You couldn't miss the two men walking down the first fairway on the warm Tuesday morning. The shorter man, highly regarded in the financial sector, walked with a focused intensity, as was his custom. The other man couldn't hide even if he wanted to, a fact not solely attributed to his towering height: across the world he was already thought of as perhaps the greatest player ever to pick up a basketball.

Their golf outing had taken quite some time to arrange. Michael Jordan, in the middle of his dynastic run with the Chicago Bulls, always saw his basketball season end well into the summer. Francis Leo Kirby, or FL as he is known, had donated a round of golf with himself and the recently crowned world champion as part of a charity event. Though the demands on his time had grown considerably, Michael had still made the outing a priority.

They walked to the first tee where two of FL's children, Kelley and Kasey, would have the honor of serving as caddies for their basketball hero. Before teeing off, the two men agreed to a friendly wager and soon found themselves on the first green. As FL stood over his ball, Jordan, ever the competitor and always seeking an edge, asked FL, "Hey, Kirby. Have you ever in your life had to make a big shot?"

FL looked up, eyes narrowing.

"Hey, Michael . . ." he offered. The other players in the group couldn't hear the rest of his comments, but Michael certainly did. Michael replied, dropped his head sheepishly, and nodded to FL in a gesture of respect. It was an uncommon reaction from a man whose competitive ferocity and withering glares had stopped many an opponent (and a few teammates) in their tracks. But Michael Jordan had just heard something on the golf course he had never heard on a basketball court. It would be many years before FL told anyone outside his family exactly what was said.

Exmoor Country Club is tucked quietly away in a modest residential neighborhood. It has a deep history going back to the late 1800s. Tree-lined and slightly undulating, the course is shaped and maintained to take advantage of Mother Nature's gifts. In this environment of proud history and humble success, FL Kirby is viewed with a quiet reverence. You can feel it in the way people greet him, the way they stand and shake his hand, and the way they whisper and nod in his direction after he walks away. You would be wrong to assume it was his professional success. Someone will have to tell you the reason behind the reverence, because he would never volunteer it.

FL was raised in a small town, west of Boston. His childhood was typical in many ways. Watched over by an overprotective mother and hardworking father, he gravitated to youth sports because, as an only child, he enjoyed the camaraderie that football, hockey, and baseball provided.

Often he would sit on the front lawn watching Air Force planes depart from a nearby airfield. "I wonder where they are going," he thought. His fondest memories of those early years were of the times spent with his dad. He worked for New England Telephone and would often take young FL with him on different jobs he had to tackle. Other times FL would travel with his dad on weekends to help with janitorial work at a local bank. One particular memory stands out for FL: watching his dad leave to climb utility poles on Christmas morning to repair broken telephone lines. FL saw how hard his dad worked, and it left a lasting impression on him.

FL embodied this work ethic as he entered his high school years. He split time washing dishes at the local hospital and working at the beach during the day before going to the General Motors assembly line at night. Another memorable job was making salad dressing at Ken's Steakhouse. Work was simply a way of life for FL. He continued to enjoy childhood sports, but hockey became his primary sport, and he played it with fearless abandon, helping his team win the state championship his junior year. Still, FL, who wasn't a great student and was by his own admission a bit unfocused, did not know what he wanted to do upon graduation from high school. What he did know was that regardless of what he was going to do, he needed more discipline and better study habits.

But he had come from a family with a deep commitment to military service. His dad was one of three sons who served in World War II, all at the same time. One of those boys would not return. The military influence of the elder Kirby took young FL to Norwich University, the military college in Vermont founded in 1819. At this esteemed institution, FL continued to play hockey and stay out of trouble, although he was more successful in achieving the former. But soon enough the mission of Norwich University—"to make moral, patriotic, efficient, and useful citizens, and to qualify them for all those high responsibilities resting upon a citizen of this free republic"—began to sink in.[1]

In his junior year, FL was selected, along with eleven others, to attend Air Force ROTC flight school. Though he had never been in a plane before, he thought he might enjoy the experience because his dad had piloted a Douglas DC-3 carrying paratroopers for the invasion of Normandy on June 6, 1944. The young boy who sat on the lawn studying airplanes through his binoculars was now going to be up close and personal.

FL Kirby graduated from Norwich University in 1966 and was asked by his former teacher to teach a modern math class to seventh and eighth graders. He'd never taken modern math, let alone taught a class, but accepted the challenge and taught for four months before he had to enter the army. His first day of class, he gathered the class together and said,

"I might know less about this subject than you do, but I bet if we tackle it together, we can learn something."

In January 1967, FL departed for Fort Knox in Kentucky for basic training. He was classified as an armor officer, which meant he might end up as a tank commander. But the month before, the secretary of defense had mandated that the army needed more helicopter pilots. FL's prior Air Force ROTC training assured him of going to helicopter training. With his basic training completed, FL then headed to Mineral Wells, Texas, for flight school. Here he learned airmanship skills, from hovering and landing to executing emergency procedures. He also learned that he was to start training for combat in Vietnam. It was now April 1967.

In August of the same year, his training now completed, FL and eleven others were chosen from among thousands to convert Hunter Air Force Base in Savannah, Georgia, into an army helicopter base, known as Hunter Army Airfield. At Hunter they underwent Advanced Training and were scheduled to graduate in December 1967.

FL had performed perfectly throughout his training up to the final flight physical exam, which he failed: his EKG showed a heartbeat abnormality. He pleaded to the flight surgeon, a captain, that he had to graduate. "My parents are on a flight right now from Boston to Savannah to see their only child graduate. I've been through all this training, and I've already passed all the other flight exams, and I've been rated; you have to let me graduate!" Thinking quickly, FL asked if the condition was a grounding one, since he was already rated. The captain said it was not. They agreed to a compromise: FL could graduate but would have to take another EKG. If he passed, he could keep his hard-earned wings. The second time, he did pass the physical, and his duty to country in the US Army continued.

In January 1968, FL headed to Vietnam. To this day, FL thinks about how difficult that must have been for his parents to send an only child off to war. His father had already seen a brother not return from World War II. Even his name was a concession to the uncertainty of war. FL's mother did not want to name him after his father, Francis Leo, but was convinced only when her friends and family told her that if her husband did not survive the war in Europe, the name should carry on. She conceded the point but only with the condition that it be shortened to FL. But still, the elder Kirby's length of service in World War II meant he would not see his firstborn son until he was one and a half years old.

As FL prepared to leave home, his parents were well aware that he might not return. In the eyes of many Americans, Vietnam was no longer a minor skirmish in another part of the world but a major conflict with no end. For those who doubted that sobering fact, front-page headlines of national newspapers had begun daily reporting of casualties. FL would learn that to deal with the uncertainty of war, his father, who was not a churchgoer, began going to church and would continue to do so for the rest of his life. He was accompanied by FL's mother, who had always been anxious about FL's well-being but never more than when he was half a world away.

The flight to Vietnam was long and arduous. A flight to San Francisco, then to Hawaii for refueling, and next to the Philippines, specifically Clark Air Base on Luzon Island. From there they would fly into Vietnam. The length of the journey gave FL a lot of time to think. "What am I getting into?" he wondered. His thoughts were interrupted by an announcement from the pilot: they were going to be held at Clark indefinitely. All the bases in Vietnam were under attack, and there was no safe way to approach. Facing an enemy with the capacity to attack multiple bases awakened FL to a harsh reality: he was not stepping into a small conflict but a full-blown war.

He and his unit would live at the terminals for seven days. Then they heard the sirens signaling it was time to board for the final leg of their journey to Vietnam. The flight to Saigon, and Tan Son Nhut Air Base, would be nearly three hours. As they neared Saigon, the pilot came over the radio: "The airport is under attack. When we land, buses will be waiting. Get on the buses quickly and get down on the floor. They will take you to the in-country center." What FL and the others did not know was that they had arrived in Vietnam as preparations were under way for the Tet Offensive. This coordinated attack against the US and her allies saw eighty-five thousand Vietcong and North Vietnamese fighters descend on valuable targets in southern Vietnam. One of their main targets was Tan Son Nhut Air Base, where FL and his recruits had just landed.

They finally made it to the in-country center and checked in. FL was designated as a member of the 3rd Squadron of the 11th Armored Cavalry Regiment. Five days in country, he boarded a plane, alone, headed to what would be his base camp, Blackhorse. FL saw his flight school roommate,

Dave Moss, heading out in a jeep with a flak jacket on and a machine gun in his hand. Neither knew where the other was headed.

FL soon discovered his base camp was fifteen miles east of Saigon. When they landed, he found himself standing alone on a runway going east to west. No one came to greet him, nor could he see anyone. Ever since landing in Vietnam, he was unaware of the uncertainty of its outcome, and now staring down the runway in the middle of the jungle, he experienced yet another wave of doubt. As the plane departed, he picked up his duffel bag and headed to the south side of the runway. Finally, he saw someone, who showed him to a small tent hut, commonly referred to as a hooch.

Inside, there were several inches of thick, red dust on his bed. Four other beds were crammed inside the hooch. He headed to check-in and received his weapons, an M14 and a .45 pistol, and loads of ammunition. FL listened intently as his commanding officer told him he wouldn't be going into the field for a few weeks and that essentially he would be by himself.

"Where is everybody? What happens if we come under attack?"

He realized he had said the words aloud when he heard the answer: "We never get attacked here." He was directed to dinner, which was really World War II C-rations. After he ate, he headed to the officers' club, which was nothing more than a tent with a noncommissioned officer inside tending bar. FL sat drinking, alone in his thoughts.

He finally headed back to the hooch, cleaning away the

layers of red dust, and lay down on his bed, clothes on. Suddenly, in the quiet of night, came a resounding boom. It was followed by a series of incoming mortar rounds and screeching sirens; the camp that had never come under attack was suddenly being targeted. Staggering out of the hooch, FL headed to the perimeter of the camp where an earth wall would offer some defense against the attack. Though he couldn't see in the dark, he was shooting anyway. At worst it would scare away the snakes and rats, which Vietnam was known for and of which he was deathly afraid. At best he would get the enemy. After what seemed like an eternity, but in reality was only an hour, the shooting stopped, the sirens sounded, and it was all over.

The following morning came, and FL was due for his in-country check ride with a helicopter instructor. It was required that he go out in the field as soon as possible, and soon they were seated in the mechanical bird. Seated in the passenger seat, soaring through the Vietnamese sky, FL was again struck by the beautiful landscape of the country and its seemingly serene environment. The checkout pilot showed him the various checkpoints and other spots he would need to know. As they headed back, FL was required to perform some emergency procedures, but first the checkout pilot wanted to demonstrate how to execute an autorotation to land the helicopter with no power. In flight school FL had done it thousands of times; in training they were drilled on it every day.

They approached the runway, and the instructor lined up the helicopter, with about eight hundred feet to go. The instructor rolled off the throttle. The autorotation procedure requires the pilot to perform a complicated maneuver in which they use air flow to turn the rotors instead of the engine.

As they came to the runway touchdown, the helicopter started to skid off the runway. The instructor looked at FL and said, "We must have hit a wind shear. Let's go again." They tried again, and this time everything was set up perfectly. The instructor lined up for touchdown once again, but this time the nose of the helicopter suddenly dove left so quickly that the instructor did not have time to react. The helicopter bounced and then rolled over twice, filling the world with the sounds of screeching metal and snapping rotor blades. "Everything went into slow motion," FL remembers.

When the helicopter finally came to a stop, FL could hear the blare of the sirens as fire trucks rushed to the scene. Miraculously, FL was unharmed, but the instructor seriously injured his back. The inquiry found the instructor had failed to test full travel with the pedals, resulting in a right pedal setup that caused the pedal to hit the radio box. Without full travel, the instructor was unable to turn the nose to the right. It was not, as the instructor suspected, wind shear, but an accident. The instructor, who had only a few weeks left in Vietnam, was sent home, his service complete.

Within forty-eight hours of landing at base camp, FL had come under attack and had been involved in a helicopter accident. It was a long way from his Massachusetts hometown and basic training. Francis Leo Kirby was in a real war.

FL settled into a routine if there was such a thing in

Vietnam. The work was hard and unforgiving. The South Vietnamese, who the Americans were supporting, had little training and were terrible fighters. US soldiers lived life in the field, always on the alert for any sign of the enemy. They slept in tents, in helicopters, or against a tank, but they never really rested. Vietnam is a tropical rainforest and provides nothing but relentless humidity. Meanwhile, the faceless enemy used guerilla warfare tactics like spike pits and booby traps. They were adept at setting ambushes and hiding in plain sight. American soldiers' greatest fear was getting captured, because the enemy was known to torture Americans, breaking their bodies, their spirits, or both. They witnessed the loss of many good men who died thousands of miles from home, fighting in a war that was growing increasingly unpopular back home. They were surrounded by the anxiety and fear of others, as well as their own.

FL's helicopter squadron called themselves the Bandits, and FL was known as Bandit 16. The role of the helicopter pilot in Vietnam was varied: flying scout surveillance, providing logistics support and combat assault support, extracting the wounded. In every instance, they expected to be shot at, and they were rarely wrong. One particular time, a platoon was under ambush, taking enemy fire from a hidden location. FL, in a "Loach" (a scout helicopter) with a colonel on board and his door gunner inside with fifteen hundred rounds of ammunition, was headed to talk to the commander of the platoon to gather intelligence on the enemy's last known position. The Loach was easily maneuverable, and FL landed without incident. He talked to the platoon leader briefly, but as he was departing to locate the enemy, eleven North Vietnamese soldiers suddenly emerged from the trees and fired on the helicopter. There was no longer a need to find the enemy because the enemy had found them.

Always on alert, FL spotted them first and shouted to the gunner, "Open fire!" while striking the left pedal quickly to get the gunner into position. The helicopter was taking heavy fire, but the door gunner reacted quickly to FL's command, striking every one of the enemy soldiers. The last one took a round to the knee and went down, but not before he fired his rocket-propelled grenade. Acting quickly and instinctively, FL maneuvered the helicopter just enough as the rocket passed beneath them, so close they could see the round go by. In seconds, they had not only confirmed the location of the enemy but had eliminated the threat, if only barely.

When they finally gathered themselves from the close call, they realized the barrel of the gun had become so hot, it had bent and would not have been able to fire another round. The gunner was awarded a Bronze Star that very day.

One particular battle is seared in FL's memory. It occurred at Duc Hoa, a rural district of the Long An province in the Mekong Delta region. FL's squadron had set up a perimeter of tanks and armored personnel carriers on a steep hillside. Suddenly, the sound of .50-caliber machine guns filled the air. The enemy was firing on them from all directions, pinning the squadron on the hillside. But the gunfire gave away the location of the enemy, and FL called in repeated air strikes on their position. Unbeknownst to the Americans, the North Vietnamese were holed up in concrete bunkers seemingly invulnerable to the bombardment. For two weeks, the assault continued with no effect. With US soldiers unable to advance, the situation was growing dire.

It seemed the air strikes were only strengthening, not weakening, the enemy. The men talked among themselves. "What kind of enemy is this? Who can withstand that kind of bombardment?" In an effort to alleviate that anxiety, FL sought out his squadron commander. "The men's nerves are frayed. Morale is low. We need to do something."

"What do you suggest?" his commander asked. FL already had an idea in mind: he would fly to Củ Chi, north of Saigon, some twenty miles away, to pick up a chaplain. Any denomination would do. It was an unorthodox request, but the commander agreed, knowing that the men needed a lift. Neither FL nor the chaplain would make it back to the hillside in Duc Hoa.

Before climbing into the helicopter, FL armed himself with two bandoliers of ammunition, a grenade launcher, an M14, and a .38 pistol. In midflight there was a sudden loud bang, and FL realized his engine had gone out; his helicopter no longer had power. All his training on how to land a helicopter without power kicked in, including the helicopter crash when he first arrived in Vietnam. To this day he does not know if he was hit or if it was engine failure.

"Mayday, Mayday," he called out on the universal channel. "Bandit 16 going down." He went through the appropriate protocols. He gave the coordinates of his approximate location, keeping his voice even and steady, without emotion, purposefully disguising the enormous danger he was suddenly in. This was what he had been trained to do.

FL calmly worked the pedals to set down the helicopter upright, landing in a rice paddy field. Had it rolled, as it had during his training exercise, he could have been seriously injured or given away his location. Once the enemy saw the helicopter, they would immediately start looking for him. He knew he had to get away from the helicopter as soon as possible, and he did, sprinting away until it was nothing more than a speck in the distance.

From the sky, rice paddy fields in Vietnam appear as a beautiful quilt of interlaced green patterns. On the ground and in the midst of war, they are far more sinister. The elephant-tall grass hides booby traps and land mines and enemy fighters waiting to ambush an unsuspecting patrol. But now for FL, it offered an unlikely place to hide while he determined what to do next.

Hiding in a rice dike and halfway submerged in a small stream, FL assessed his position. He had issued the Mayday distress call but had no way of knowing if it had been received. He had gone down behind enemy lines, between Duc Hoa and Củ Chi. This was the epicenter for the underground tunnel networks that the Vietcong had used so effectively against the US soldiers. Though it was quiet, and he saw none of the enemy nor any villagers who could give him away, that could change at any moment.

At the forefront of FL's mind was the possibility of capture. Like his fellow soldiers, he had heard the many stories of what happened to prisoners, including a soldier in his unit who had gone insane while in captivity. The Vietcong did not abide by the rules of the Geneva Convention, which held that all prisoners of war be treated humanely. Rather, barbaric torture in dimly lit dungeons filled with snakes and rats awaited these soldiers. That was only if they survived the brutal trek to northern prison camps.

FL was certain he would die and the only say he had left was in how. He had a plan. He had thought of the war movies he'd seen where a trapped soldier would deliberately fire on a large enemy platoon, knowing full well that he was outmanned and that their return fire would kill him. If that tactic did not work, he had already counted the amount of ammunition he had. He would fire on any enemy that came his way until he had one bullet left, and that one would be for himself. In no universe was FL going to allow himself to be captured and then tortured beyond human understanding.

He glanced at his watch and mentally cataloged the time. "Right about now, my mom and dad are sitting down to dinner with no idea that their only child is going to die. I hope I made you proud. I hope you know I fought the good fight."

FL kept asking, "God, why am I here? Give me a plan." He stopped short of making a deal with God; the God he prays to does not deal in barters and transactions. For three long hours, which felt more like lifetimes, FL lay in a water-filled paddy field, looking for any sign of the enemy, thinking about his parents and praying to God for the strength to handle whatever fate would befall him.

Suddenly he heard the roar of two gunships approaching and knew immediately that these were American; the North Vietnamese did not use helicopters in-country. He popped a can of smoke, the yellow plumes floating into the air, to signal his location. As one of them approached, he stood up with outstretched hands over his head, as if giving homage to this mechanical god that had come to save him. He climbed aboard while gunners flanked the open doors of the helicopter, on alert for any sign of the enemy.

What those airships were doing in that area at that time FL never learned. Nor did he find out if they were looking for him; but they had found him and saved his life. As they flew back to his encampment, he sat in the back seat looking at the two pilots and the door gunners, pondering what had just unfolded. "Why me? Why am I being saved?" He had known many who were not, those who paid the ultimate price. How true that was not even FL fully knew. Twelve thousand helicopters went into service in Vietnam, and by the end of the war, almost half would be lost—along with nearly five thousand pilots and crew members.

When FL returned to his squadron, they ferried a helicopter from the base camp so he could continue to fly. The next day he was flying missions again. There was no time to consider what had happened, and the army didn't want him to. The rule was that you went back up as soon as possible.

For the next year, FL would continue to fly missions. There were successful and unsuccessful missions, lives saved and lives lost. He's never forgotten those who were lost, and while he knows he did everything he could, a part of him still wonders if he could have done something more.

On January 4, 1969, FL had completed his tour of duty in Vietnam. For those who had served, the name of the aircraft that would bring them home had particular meaning: the *Freedom Bird*. As he sat in the briefing room, waiting to board, FL listened quietly as the major advised the servicemen: "Gentlemen, when you get home, the antiwar demonstrators are heavy. If anyone asks if you have been to Vietnam, you are wise to say no."

On the *Freedom Bird*, FL had a window seat. Pondering his service, he asked himself what was different from the day he arrived. The war was poorly executed. FL reminisces, "It was 'capture that hill,' and then once we did, we left it behind only to have to come back and do it again. What was the ultimate mission?" There seemed to be none. All he could see were a bunch of lives lost and families forever altered, but nothing else had changed. As he was departing, he could see new soldiers coming into his base camp, destined to face exactly what he had.

FL soon found what the major had said about the antiwar movement to be true. Wanting to surprise his parents, he took a red-eye flight from San Francisco to Logan Airport in Boston. When he deplaned, a man walking alongside him looked at his uniform and asked menacingly, "Are you one of those Vietnam guys?"

FL had served in Vietnam to answer the call of his country, as his father had before him. He had done so under orders, and those orders were to be followed. But this point was going to be lost on his judgmental interrogator. Rather than have a debate, FL said simply, "No, that was not me." A man who had put his life on the line for his country had to deny that he had ever done so.

The brave soldiers who fought on the front lines in Vietnam don't often volunteer what that experience was like. Perhaps it is because of some of the residue of risking their lives for an unpopular war or their inability to fully capture the devastation of warfare. It is this way with FL as well—unless of course a basketball hero unknowingly questions whether you understand what it means to perform under pressure.

"Hey, Michael," he had replied that warm summer morning. "Have you ever tried to land a helicopter to save your fellow soldiers while you have the enemy shooting at you?"

"No," the greatest player in the world responded, "can't say I have."

"Well," FL said, pointing down at his golf ball decorated with a Bandit 16 logo, "I kinda knew that already. Because if you had, you'd know this is not really a big shot." Jordan nodded in complete agreement.

First Lieutenant Francis L. Kirby is the recipient of some of the highest medals the nation can bestow on an airman, including the Distinguished Flying Cross and the Bronze Star Medal. One line in the description of the former catches the eye: "Despite many adversities, First Lieutenant Kirby invariably performed his duties in a resolute and efficient manner." Years later, long after he thought he had already seen his greatest battle, FL would be required to call on those same qualities again.

The Lighthouse Effect: The Courage to Encourage

We have come to identify courage mostly as acts of bravery demonstrated by a single individual: a firefighter runs into a burning building to save a life, a Good Samaritan leaps onto train tracks to rescue a distressed traveler, a lifeguard battles vicious riptides to pull a struggling swimmer to safety. We admire their willingness to put themselves in jeopardy to save a life and point out their sacrifices to others as examples of what we should all strive to do.

The lighthouse is the ideal image for the physical representation of courage. As a lighthouse stretches toward the sky, majestic in appearance, your eye can't help but be drawn to the aura of this architectural marvel and the compelling picture of strength it provides. But it is when the storm rages that we fully understand the courage the lighthouse represents. When the sea becomes a tempestuous beast, the lighthouse transforms into an urgent beacon signaling the way toward shelter, courageously defying the elements.

When you look at those acts of bravery, you might think that courage is defined only by the extraordinary feat. Few of us, on a daily basis, are required to summon the kind of courage that FL Kirby had to when his helicopter went down. But there were smaller examples of FL's courage too. When he went to his squadron leader to tell him that the men needed a spiritual lift, he was doing so knowing that his commanding officer could reject the idea or even reprimand him.

Each day offers you an opportunity to overcome obstacles and fears in your life. Those victories, however small they appear, are significant and don't need to be measured against or compared with those of someone else. They stand on their own as important measures of your own personal capabilities. When you speak up during a meeting, challenge herd thinking, establish rules for how you will be treated, or overcome a fear of public speaking, you create patterns of courage that will ultimately become habit. The following ideas are ways you can be courageous in your everyday life.

Preparation Is Power

When you face uncertainty or fear, somewhere in the cause of that concern is a nagging feeling that you are not fully prepared. You can imagine that when FL first heard the sound of the helicopter's engine failing, he felt fear and anxiety. But just as quickly he turned to the skills he had developed in training; he was prepared for this possibility and responded accordingly. In addition, he also called upon a prior setback, the crash during his training experience, to help guide him. Your own setbacks aren't what they first appear to be; rather than viewing them as failures, view them as learning opportunities that are the building blocks for future preparation.

Make the Leap

No words said or written can erase this fact: at some point you are going to have to make a leap. It will be scary because every leap has some element of uncertainty. *What if I fail?* But independent of the outcome, there will still be lessons you can take from the risk. There is something else for you to consider, an emotion that might be stronger than the fear you battle: regret. Regret is such a powerful feeling because it often stays with us for days, months, or even years, reminding us of something we could have done or should have done. As a regular part of your life, you should always ask, What would I attempt to do if I knew I could not fail or would not disappoint? Fear of failing or disappointing is frequently the obstacle that gets in the way of taking a risk, and subsequently building courage. Write down your answer to that question, and put it somewhere you will come across it every day, whether it be your bathroom mirror or the background of your cell phone.

Encourage

Courage is not only about finding bravery for ourselves. It is also about helping others find theirs. There is a word for this: *encourage*, which means "to make strong, or hearten."[2] The very nature of this definition means that courage is not focused on you but rather what you can offer to others.

Tell Me More

When someone shares a desire or a dream, remember back to a time when you wanted to stretch beyond a perceived limitation. You can almost certainly recall your concerns and reservations about that risk. What you most needed then is likely what your friend, colleague, or family member needs now. In trusting you with that dream, they are asking you to be their lighthouse. You are in a unique position to light their path and further empower them. When I was thinking about writing my first book, I called a friend, Doug Hardy, who spent some time in the publishing industry. The entire process seemed daunting, and I was not convinced that my journey, while important to me, would be of interest to anyone else. We sat down for lunch, and when I initially shared my story with Doug, he responded simply by saying, "Tell me more." That simple phrase—"tell me more"—was exactly the encouragement I needed to overcome my uncertainty. When FL went to his squadron leader to tell him that the men needed a spiritual lift, his commanding officer responded by asking, "What do you suggest?"

Offer Solutions

Offering encouragement does not mean blindly supporting one's aspirations with false optimism. Not at all. Should you have concerns about what they're trying to accomplish, you can be most helpful by sharing your concerns *and suggesting ways to address them.* To simply share your concerns without offering solutions puts you in the role of the cynical critic rather than the helpful guide. Rather, you can offer constructive guidance and helpful support: "Can I make a suggestion? How about if you tried it this way? What are our options?"

When someone we know is afraid of judgment, we can provide a safe haven for their hopes by telling them first and foremost that we are proud of their efforts. In doing so, we are recognizing the risk they are taking and the vulnerability they might be feeling. Being proud of their effort is not predicated on a successful outcome but rather in acknowledging the attempt they are making. We can remind them that anytime you step outside of someone else's expectations for your life, there is likely to be a judgment. But those opinions are reflections of what *they* think is possible for you and not what *you* think is possible for you. We can remind them that we can't walk through the world carrying the heavy burden of someone else's chains of what our life should be or how it should be lived.

As I was writing this book, and spending time with these human lighthouses, I began to see the many things they held in common. One of them was in their willingness to share the painful journeys of their lives. There is a vulnerability one feels when doing so; part of you relives the difficulty of your own storm all over again. But I learned that these seemingly ordinary people were willing to do so because they hope someone might take encouragement from their experiences. This is especially true for FL Kirby, whose demonstration of courage would continue long after he left the battlefield of Vietnam.

Two years ago the Kirby family was gathered in Florida for Thanksgiving dinner. Their son Kris had a particularly hard flight from Minnesota, where he lived, battling a snowstorm and a six-hour flight delay to get there. Judy, FL's wife of the last four decades, had set aside leftovers, which Kris polished off quickly while the family gathered around him. They caught up for a bit on the front porch before Kris headed off to bed, exhausted from his travels. But early the next morning Kris awoke and, after spending some time talking with his mom, went off for a jog in the warm morning sun. FL had already left the house, driving past the security gate, headed for a workout at the local gym.

As FL was returning, he passed a group of ambulances and emergency personnel just down the street from the Kirby home. He pulled over and asked the small crowd that had gathered what was happening. "Not sure," came the reply. "We think someone collapsed." FL pulled into the driveway and walked inside to tell Judy about the commotion down the street.

Judy stopped him. "Kris has been gone a long time."

They called the guard at the security gate and described Kris.

"We aren't sure, but it could be him," the answer came.

"Is he still there?" they inquired.

"No," came the reply.

They headed to the emergency room at the nearest hospital. When they identified themselves, they were escorted to a tiny room. To anyone who wore a white uniform they would stop and ask, "Where is Kris? What are they doing? Why is everyone acting so strange?"

Moments later they were told the horrible news: Kris had passed away of a massive heart attack. He was just forty-four years old, leaving behind three young children.

The pain in FL's voice is raw and apparent as he describes this tragic series of events. "I wanted to exchange my life for his that day. You raise your kids expecting them to graduate high school and college, marry, have children of their own, and find a career they really enjoy. You can't believe something like this can happen."

FL continues, "Kris was a great son and a great dad. He was asked to give the commencement speech at Bethel College when he graduated, not because he was magna cum laude but because of what he meant to the students and faculty there. Kris loved fishing, and his whole speech to the class was on the lures of life. It was an amazing speech for a guy his age. Me and Judy could have never been prouder."

In the face of such an indescribable loss, FL and Judy have had to call upon a new kind of courage that begins with their deep and abiding faith. The love and support of their friends and extended family has also been invaluable because even lighthouses need lighthouses. There is no such thing as moving on, but you do have to move forward because the world will, whether you do or not. But the Kirbys have chosen to do so in a particular way by becoming a resource for others who have also suffered the unexpected loss of a loved one. These families are looking for comfort and guidance and a way to bring meaning to their lives again. You can imagine that the conversations are tough for FL and Judy because they are reminders that their beloved Kris left them so suddenly. It can take a particular courage to encourage another, but the Kirbys understand that even our deepest struggles can be a lighthouse for someone else.

Sometimes I see FL on the driving range of the golf course with his grandchildren. He stands back and watches quietly, offering a tip or two that is more likely to be about life than about the game. I wave from a distance, knowing not to intrude but smiling quietly to myself nevertheless. One day soon the grandchildren will learn about the bravery and the courage of their grandfather.

CHAPTER 4

GREG ANTHONY

Our fate is to face the world as orphans,
chasing through long years the shadows
of vanished parents. There is nothing for
it but to try and see through our missions
to the end, as best we can, for until we
do so, we will be permitted no calm.
—KAZUO ISHIGURO

Several years ago I requested my case file from the Massachusetts Department of Social Services. It was a long and bureaucratic process, but that didn't particularly bother me. By then I'd met most of the Pemberton and Murphy families, heard the stories of my mother and father, and figured that I already knew everything I needed to know about my early childhood years. I turned out to be quite wrong about that.

As I was reading through the large file, a faded color photo fell from its pages. It landed picture-side up, and on it appeared a young boy about seven or eight years old. His eyes were a bluish-green, and he wore a patterned blue-and-white shirt with a collar so large it made him appear as if he did not have a neck. "They've put another child's photo in my case file," I thought. "I'll have to mail this back."

I flipped it over, looking for any identifying information, and saw the unexplainable: my birth name, Steve Klakowicz. "Really?" I thought. I turned it back over to look at the picture again. "That's me?" I had never seen a picture of me as a young boy, and to the best of my knowledge no such picture existed. To see one, then in my midthirties, left me speechless.

The longer I stared at the photo, the more the details of the picture came flooding back. I remembered a social worker had brought me to Buttonwood Park in the west end of the city of New Bedford. She had let me explore all the fun contraptions, and I had gravitated to the swing set. She stopped me while I was trying to swing to the heavens and snapped my picture. The childhood joy of being in a park, and of having my picture taken for the first time, was captured in my gleeful expression in a photo that had lain dormant in my case file for thirty years. By the time the picture was taken, I was, in the eyes of the family court, an orphan.

There are generally considered two types of orphans, biological and social. A biological orphan is a child who has no living parent. A social orphan has parents who are living but are unable to provide for their child, so the child must find sanctuary elsewhere. The United States has an all-encompassing definition that includes both meanings: "a minor bereft through death or disappearance of, abandonment or desertion by, separation or loss from, both parents."[1] No one could have told you exactly what group I belonged to because my father had not been publicly identified, not by my mother or the social services system. My mother's whereabouts were unknown, and her social workers speculated that even if she was alive, it would not be for much longer, given her difficulties. No one, including her own family, thought it would be a good idea for me to be returned to her.

The night I was taken from my mother, I was brought to St. Mary's Home, an orphanage located on Kempton Street. I would not be there long; the desire to find me a permanent home was a reflection of an ongoing shift away from orphanages and toward foster care and state-supported care of dependent children. In the mid-1800s there were estimated to be one thousand orphanages in the US, housing over one hundred thousand children. Today orphanages, at least how we have historically defined them, no longer exist.

The concept of the orphan has been with us since ancient times. In the Bible, the word *orphan* is mentioned twenty-seven times. Charles Dickens wrote frequently of orphans, from *Oliver Twist* to *Great Expectations*. For thirty years *Annie* held the record as the longest running show on Broadway. One of the most popular holiday movies of all time, *Home Alone*, tells the story of a young Kevin McCallister, who is orphaned—albeit temporarily and unintentionally—by his parents. Batman, Spider-Man, and Superman have different superpowers but one particular thing in common: they are all orphans—as were Cinderella, Jane Eyre, Frodo Baggins, Harry Potter, and James Bond. The list goes on.

We have alternatingly mythologized and romanticized the idea of the orphan. As parents we place these stories in our children's lives so they can develop empathy and gratitude and perhaps as a last-ditch strategy to get them to clean up their rooms. As young children we are drawn to the orphan narrative because though these fictional orphans are similar to us in age, they had to become adults sooner, often outsmarting or defying real adults along the way. They had a freedom and a secret kind of strength we long for.

The real picture of orphans in the world is an entire universe away from the mythologized versions that have sunk into our consciousness. The numbers are so astonishing, you have to do a double take to make sure you are reading them correctly: there are 140 million orphans in the world, a number that grows by 5,700 *each* day. Ninety-five percent of them are over the age of five. In the United States, there are nearly 450,000 children in foster care, and 117,000 of them are waiting to be adopted. Over half will spend anywhere from two to five years in the foster care system. For older children, each year 23,000 of them will "age out," which means that when the kids reach their eighteenth birthday, society believes it has met its commitment to them, and they are no longer eligible to receive any type of support.[2] It is no accident that many of these young people, who have just left one system, find themselves part of another: homelessness, addiction, and incarceration.

Orphans exist in a world marked by questions and uncertainty: Where have I come from? Who do I look like? Where are my mother and father? When are they coming for me? A cloud of wandering hangs over them: various placements, numerous social workers, and frequent school transfers. The one thing they know for certain is that nothing is certain.

They are always on the lookout for someone to pull them out of this ambiguous existence. A teacher who offers them something other than a dead-eyed smile of pity or a social worker who uses their name when they talk to them might be the person to provide them sanctuary. Whenever they see anything that approaches a normal family, they imagine going home with them, being seated at their dinner table, and being part of their family. When they hear people complain about growing up in a single-parent household, their real reaction is one of envy. *So you had one parent?*

Whatever orphans lack in normalcy, they make up for in resiliency. They pay attention to detail; they anticipate challenges and take nothing for granted. Still, it is hard to trust anyone; they survive by knowing that they're almost certainly going to be let down, and they're best prepared if they simply expect it.

Greg Anthony was born into a large family in Tiverton, Rhode Island. There were thirteen siblings in all, and Greg, the last boy, fell into the younger group. As the youngest boy, he found himself on the receiving end of his older brothers' entertainment, including one memorable time when they put him in a potato sack and rolled him down a flight of stairs. Clothes and shoes were handed down from one child to the next. Their mother was a stay-at-home mom, and their father was a draftsman trying to provide for the family as best he could.

Tragedy struck the family often. One of the siblings died in a car accident, and another during a failed operation. Being part of a large family allowed them to endure these heartbreaks with some degree of support because, while they did not have much, they still had each other—until they didn't.

One particular evening, when Greg was three years old, a fire broke out in the attic of their small home on Crandall Road. It was the second fire in several months, but the second one was so severe that the house was no longer livable. It would have devastating consequences for the family. With no means to create an alternative living situation, his parents made a decision regarding the younger children: they would have to be sent to orphanages. Greg and one set of twins went to Mount St. Francis orphanage in Woonsocket, and the three brothers closest to him in age went to a different orphanage in another part of the state. Greg heard later on that his older brothers kept running away from the orphanage back to the place where their mother lived.

Greg's introduction to orphanage life was harsh. The staff first cut off all his hair, and he bolted away, running down the hill as fast as his little legs could carry him. They sent the janitor after three-year-old Greg to retrieve him and bring him back to Mount St. Francis. On his return, they put him in a crib with the rails up so he couldn't get out. And it worked because he never ran away again. Still, he was defiant and often found himself on the receiving end of discipline, including being dunked naked in a tub of cold water. This didn't quite have the effect they hoped for—young Greg loved the cold water.

At Greg's new residence, the boys and girls were separated, and though Greg knew his sisters were there, he rarely saw them. On the occasions he did, it was through a chain-link fence that separated the play areas. When the three of them spied each other, they would run to the fence and lock fingers through the rusty divider.

This was the only family contact Greg would have during his time in the orphanage. He has no recollection of visits from his mother or father.

After a few years, with no contact from his parents, Greg and his sisters were sent to another orphanage, St. Aloysius in Greenville, Rhode Island. When he arrived at the second orphanage, the other boys devised an initiation: Greg would have to get in the boxing ring and fight bigger kids. They underestimated the new arrival, however, and were unaware that he was prepared to fight to the bitter end. They kept sending someone older and older until finally a boy much older got the best of him. Still, he had sent a message: his quietness should not be interpreted as weakness.

While there, Greg became acutely ill and was hospitalized for some time. While he was in the hospital, he learned his mother had passed away. Greg doesn't remember how he and his sisters got to the funeral or back to the orphanage that day. What he does remember is seeing the mysterious figure of his father at the funeral. But there was no interaction; he can only remember seeing him.

He remembers his older brothers were there, and he recalls them challenging him to a race because they'd heard he was fast. He was still too weak to run, and though he tried, he simply couldn't keep up. He was nine years old.

As Greg entered the sixth grade, he had now been in orphanages for eight years. A prospective foster parent came to meet him and sought to become his legal guardian, but the officials at the orphanage told the foster parent that the family's wishes were that the three siblings remain together. *If you want Greg, you'll have to take his sisters as well.* Greg recalls being struck by the reference to his family. "They know I'm here," he thought. As far as he was concerned, they had forgotten about him, and that they had any feelings about him one way or another struck him as odd. Now knowing that his family knew he was there and still had not come to see him or his sisters was a hard reality to accept. So was his conclusion: *they are never going to come for us.*

The foster home functioned more like a group home, and it felt more like a form of indentured servitude than it did a family. He was required to wait on the foster mother hand and foot, and there were always many foster children in the home. Greg's plan was to graduate high school and then go out on his own where he would be free to make his own choices for the first time in his life.

One day, while coming home from a local gym, Greg saw an unfamiliar car parked at the curb. His sisters were standing there talking to a stranger through the car window. He had come to be protective of them, and he quickened his pace to get to them. When his sisters saw him, they yelled excitedly, "It's Daddy!"

He walked up to the car window, and there his father was.

"Hi, how ya' doing?" his father asked.

"Fine," Greg said quietly. An awkward silence followed, and then his father drove away. He can remember nothing else about the exchange. Greg doesn't know if he tried to come inside and his foster mom wouldn't let him in the house. He was simply there, sitting in the car for about two minutes, and then he was gone.

Greg attended private school and paid the tuition himself by working summers at the local amusement park and wherever else he could find work. While in high school, Greg became an outstanding student-athlete, and soon enough, college coaches started calling. He ultimately chose Boston University on an academic scholarship.

The next time Greg saw his father, he was in college. The siblings gathered on Thanksgiving Day at his oldest sister's home, and Greg remembers that he looked forward to going, primarily because his father would be there. They spent a few minutes quietly watching football. His father said, "I see you on TV," referring to Greg's success on the football field. It wasn't a long conversation.

As Greg was preparing to leave, his father took off the watch he was wearing and handed it to him. Greg would wear the watch every day, never taking it off. Not too long after, he was playing a game of basketball when the watch broke. When he returned home, his foster mother shared the sad news that his father had died that afternoon around three o'clock. Instinctively, Greg reached into his pocket for the broken watch and saw that it had broken right at three o'clock.

Greg went on to earn his degree in occupational therapy at Boston University. He had a little taste of the NFL with the Pittsburgh Steelers before injuries curtailed his career. He worked as an occupational therapist for a time and then returned to school for a second degree in physical therapy at the University of Connecticut while also serving as an assistant football coach.

While there, he met a fellow student, Sonja Hendrix. They saw each other every Tuesday and Thursday, as she was on the student board of governors and had office hours in the student union. As she left, Greg would be walking up the street headed toward the gym. They passed each other frequently and would say hello but did not have a meaningful conversation until they finally met at a campus party when he asked her to dance. Shortly thereafter they began dating and decided early on that their future was going to be together. They were married on a Saturday, and Sonja graduated the next day.

The happy couple lived in Rhode Island for several years before moving to Florida and then settling in Athens, Georgia, where Greg was offered the opportunity to serve as director of rehabilitation at St. Mary's Hospital. Along the way, Sonja and Greg welcomed three children into the world.

Orphans often live in the world of questions. As time and life move on, they get answers to some of them. Yet there are other questions that remain. Though he had moved forward in life, and had finally found peace in having a family of his own, Greg often wondered, "How come no one ever came to see me? Why hadn't they tried to make a connection?"

But one day, when he least expected it, someone did come looking for him.

The day I graduated from Boston College, I did so alone. There was no family to celebrate this important milestone. It had been that way for so long, I did not think it particularly odd until I walked across campus toward the ceremony and saw hundreds of families gathered around my classmates. "I came from somewhere," I thought. "Where was that place? Who were those people?" I, who had secretly wished to become a detective as a young boy, was determined to find out.

That journey for identity would take several years and many twists and turns. One of those twists found me back in my old neighborhood, standing in front of 11 Lincoln Street, where I lived with my mother for the first three years of my life. That home, a two-story colonial, was two blocks from my foster home. As a young boy, I had passed it on many occasions, unaware that a chapter in my life had unfolded in that very place.

I would also come to learn the identity of my father, once one of the top amateur fighters in the world, who had been murdered when I was five years old. He had told no one of my existence, sealing my fate as an orphan. For years, his rather large family mourned his passing, unaware he had a child. My suddenly telling them that I was Kenny Pemberton's son was quite a surprise.

When I called to tell his family who I was, they were initially skeptical. "Kenny didn't have any children, and if he did, we would have known. Why hadn't he told anyone about you?" I wanted to know the answers to those questions as much as they did. Still, whatever doubts they may have held ended as soon as they saw me in person. Though I had no memory of my father, they certainly did and knew I bore an uncanny resemblance to him.

I made it a point to meet all of Kenny's family and introduce myself. Many of them were still in New Bedford, but others had left the area. Almost a year later, I had met all his siblings except his youngest brother. As I walked up the long tree-lined walkway toward his home that spring afternoon, I was taken in by the quiet and peace of the neighborhood.

When I rang the bell, a tall brown-complexioned man answered the door. He extended his hand warmly. "Hi, I'm Greg." Greg Anthony Pemberton, the ninth of thirteen children, is my uncle.

As he ushered me into the living room, I was struck by the physical similarities between us. Perhaps it was the many years I had spent as a young boy trying to determine my identity, but seeing someone I resembled was still surreal. He introduced me to his wife, Sonja, and somewhere in the house I could hear the sounds of young children laughing while playing a game of hide-and-go-seek. Eventually they came out of their hiding spots and introduced themselves. Family pictures of Greg and Sonja with their children adorned the house. There was also a wedding photo of Greg's parents, Mary and Joseph—my grandparents.

We talked about his path to becoming a physical therapist, his college days, and how he and Sonja met. I shared the same about my own college days and my relatively new career working in higher education. We had pledged rival fraternities while at our respective universities and enjoyed some good-natured teasing about whose fraternity was better. As the conversation turned to our early years, the similarities astounded us. It was as if we'd had nearly identical childhoods, just fifteen years apart.

We'd both been separated from our mothers before the age of five. The day we left her was the last day we'd ever see her; they both passed away at the age of forty. Our fathers were either absent or distant figures in our lives, neither assuming responsibility for us. We'd spent years of our childhood waiting for family to come bring us back home. But they never did. What followed was the nomadic existence of an orphan, trying to find connection and meaning in a world that offered neither. We had both ultimately aged out of the foster care system and only a college acceptance letter averted further wandering. We belong to a rare fraternity of individuals who have never experienced what it feels like to have parents.

We've accepted that we will never fully understand some things: why his mother and father never came for him or why my father never took responsibility for me. We can dig deep into the well of justification as a way of trying to explain things to ourselves, but the truth is that there is no explanation, at least none that will be sufficient.

Some things are not our fault, but they are our responsibility. Greg and I resolved that this cycle of orphanhood and disruption, pain and loss had to end. That simple idea—that it must end—drove both of us long before we met. Nearly every life choice we made was with that goal in mind. It's why, against seemingly improbable odds, we both found a way not only to attend college in Boston—he at Boston University and I at Boston College—but also graduate and earn additional degrees. We chose careers that were more like social missions, in part because we wanted to change people's lives for the better.

Most importantly, we focused our efforts on family, understanding that a family of your own is the only thing that can ever truly fill the void of losing the family you'd been born into. To achieve that, we decided we would be the very thing we never had. We chose to be husbands and fathers even though we'd had no frame of reference for how to do that. We are not perfect, but we have tried to make a perfect effort.

When Greg and I parted the first time we met, he walked me out to my car. The kids came pouring out of the house behind him, climbing on him as if he were a human jungle gym. He was, I could tell, a natural dad—and a good one too. I thanked him for welcoming me to his home and for embracing me without reservation. He smiled gently and replied, "Well, I appreciate that, but I am the one who should be thanking you."

"Why is that?" I asked.

He paused for a moment, looking down the quiet, tree-lined street. "When I saw you walking up the driveway, it brought back memories of a time when I went looking for my family. I thought they had simply forgotten about me, and so I had to go looking for them. To have somebody seek me out, who *wanted* to find me, is a real blessing."

Over the years since we first met, Greg and I have never stopped finding each other. Maybe that's how it is for those who find family later on in life; we're always trying to make up for lost time. Our bond has grown and strengthened and has included other members of the Pemberton family. Greg and Sonja attended our wedding, and Tonya and I would do the same years later when his oldest daughter, Taryn, was married. When our first son arrived, we named him Quinn Gregory.

We gather for holidays now, and after dinner is over and the table is cleared, we bask in the glow of watching his three children and my three children enjoy one another's company. A knowing glance passes between us because we are aware of the long, hard road we traveled to create this moment. For the children, they have known only the comfort of this family, growing up in a world where there is only love and security, understanding their fathers' turbulent journeys but never experiencing them. And that's the way it should be.

The Pemberton family will continue to grow. Hundreds of years from now, we can imagine our descendants gathered together, enjoying all that family should be. Our journeys will be distant memories, if they are remembered at all. We have found peace in that truth. There is another truth too: Family is not only what you are born into. It is also who you find along the way.

The Lighthouse Effect: Uncompromising Belief

At first glance, the term *uncompromising* describes a negative behavior, commonly associated with ego, stubbornness, and an unwillingness to find middle ground. There is a lot of truth in this definition. But we all have to make compromises over the course of our lives. The challenge for many of us is to determine when we are willing to compromise and when we will not—and for what. Being uncompromising does invite uncertainty. We worry that we will be seen as too aggressive or that we are the only ones who feel a particular way about an issue. We are unwilling to draw a line for fear of judgment or being labeled a naysayer. But for Greg Pemberton, this line has always been clear.

What I have come to understand about my uncle is that his reaction to the adversity he had come upon was to fight against it. He was determined that the pain and struggle he'd experienced as a young boy would not carry forward into his adult life. He decided that he, the inheritor of a set of circumstances he neither created nor asked for, could put an end to them. To achieve that, he refused to see himself as a helpless victim blown about by the winds of chance. He would not be shackled by low expectations. Nor did he seek approval from others to determine his worth. He didn't settle for anything less than what his work ethic, sacrifice, and determination would bring him. In that sense, he was making an important statement about his own integrity, his value, and his right to find his own place in the world.

In this belief, Greg does not compromise. There is too much at stake, especially for his family. Over the years, he and Sonja have made it clear that I am part of that family. He has been as equally uncompromising about that as well, something I appreciate more than I can possibly express, especially the day I called him seeking his help.

Consider the times in your life that you needed a lighthouse and one appeared. Whoever that person was did not compromise in their belief about what was possible for you. I suspect you consider them a lighthouse because they advocated for you, extolled your virtues, or told someone about your potential. They likely directed their uncompromising belief at you as well: nudging you, challenging you, pointing out to you the greater opportunity that was in front of you. Their uncompromising belief is a large part of why it is so easy to remember our own lighthouses. Time has taught you how important they were to you. You realize that without their intervention, your life could have wound up in an alternate history, a different kind of timeline that would not have brought you to where you are today.

In many ways, your lighthouses reflect the mindset of the lighthouse keeper in the yellow rain slicker on the cover of this book. This person stands with their feet firmly planted on the lantern deck, earnestly looking out to sea for any sign of someone who might need assistance from the rapidly approaching storm. There is no negotiation or compromise in the lighthouse keepers' belief that you are worthy of being guided.

Know Your North Star

Polaris—better known as the North Star—is arguably our most well-known star. Surprisingly, this is not because of its radiance—astronomers speculate that it is not even in the top forty—but rather because of its steadiness and that it is easily identifiable. To our eye, the North Star rarely moves, and everything else in the sky appears to revolve around it.

In our lives, we need North Stars. Your North Star is

your personal mission, a goal to which you dedicate yourself and which keeps you centered and focused should you be tempted to wander. It informs the steps you take and the decisions—and the sacrifices—you are willing to make. North Stars can be short-term, long-term, or somewhere in between. Each one can be as short-term as the day ahead or a specific meeting or as long-term as ten years.

North Stars evolve over time. They are different when we are in high school, head into the workforce, or become a parent. Still, your North Stars always have the same characteristics in aligning your relationships and focusing your priorities. It helps order your steps by breaking down your life into smaller parts. You can see these goals in Greg's life. As a teenager, he worked multiple part-time jobs to save money to attend private school because he knew that would improve his chances of reaching the North Star of his life at the time: getting to college.

North Stars are the first building block of uncompromised belief. When we know what we are trying to achieve, we are less likely to be swayed by uninformed opinions and more inclined to make principled and ethical decisions. We know what will allow us to reach our North Star and what could derail us. When we find ourselves in conflict or having to make a tough decision, the North Star becomes our compass and our navigational guide, much as it did the sailors of long ago.

Protect Your Spirit

Having uncompromising belief also means safeguarding your own spirit, defining who and what you want in your life. I learned that stability matters a great deal to my uncle Greg, and he does not allow anything or anyone into his circle that takes him back to the emotions of instability that marked his early years. He does not dwell in negativity or pessimism. In the many years I have known him, I can't recall ever hearing him raise his voice or offer a disparaging word about another person.

Unfortunately, we live in a time of unprecedented toxicity. Civility seems to have faded away, and the common denominator of many interactions is rooted in rage, anger, rudeness, and shaming. Hatred has been steadily on the rise. Unlike generations past, we have to be more on the alert for things that invade our spirits, whether that be what news we digest or the relationships we have. Defining the sanctuaries that protect us matters. It could be the music we listen to, the apps we download (Calm is a particular favorite of mine), the extracurricular activities that soothe us, or the organizations we belong to. Having a place where we can simply *be*, without explanation or justification, is important.

This applies to our personal relationships as well. We can find ourselves in friendships or romantic relationships that don't lift us up but rather break us down or force us to doubt ourselves. We quietly ask ourselves, "How did I get here?" What complicates matters is that these relationships are important to us and we fear losing them.

Untie the Rope

Imagine you are standing on a bridge, connected by a loose, single rope to someone you care about. The rope represents the strong bond and connection between you. All seems well between you, but then the other person begins to pull away from you, headed in the opposite direction. You are puzzled by this and pull on the rope to get their attention; they look back at you and continue going the other way. You don't understand why, and you want to pull on the rope, but the rope is no longer loose but tight. They are dragging you in their direction. You try to dig your heels into the surface of the bridge, but you can't stop the slide. Panic rises as you realize they are now going over the side of the bridge. If you don't untie the rope, you will go over right along with them. The simple solution is to untie the rope, but there is a major dilemma in doing so: You care a great deal about this relationship, and you know they will fall. If you untie the rope, you'll feel as if you abandoned them.

What do you do? The answer is you untie the rope from yourself—and tie it to the bridge.

In doing so, you are saying that you care enough about them not to let them fall. You are also saying that you care enough about yourself and have an uncompromising belief in your own value not to go along with them. The bridge—perhaps their faith, their family, or their friends—is now their strength. What their source of strength can no longer be is you. Should they allow the bridge to be their strength and can find their way back to the top, you'll be there to reconnect, support, or find a way to tie the rope again.

Stand with Others

Uncompromising belief is not only about pushing back against something we disapprove of. It also requires us to stand *for* something, whether that be a principle, a cause, or another human being. Some of our most enduring movements in society, ones that have fundamentally changed America and made us a more inclusive society, are reflections of this very idea. At the beginning of the nineteenth century, women marched for the right to vote; fifty years later African Americans marched for the end of legal segregation and full participation in American society; people with disabilities did the same thing twenty years after that. Standing for something meaningful, positive, and for the greater good is more likely to endure than by simply saying what we are opposed to.

Often we don't speak up because we are afraid that we're the only ones who are feeling this way. We worry that we will expose ourselves to critics and judgment. But many times we are not alone in our experiences. Whenever we take a stand, we invite others who are sitting on the sidelines to join us. Those in leadership positions, whether it be in student government, teaching in the classroom, or on the board of the local parent-teacher association, can help create an environment where others can share dissenting points of view. Invite people to disagree with the majority opinion. If you're responsible for making decisions, ask people in the room what the group is *not* seeing. This protects us against groupthink or herd thinking.

Herd thinking, the tendency for individuals to blindly follow the crowd, can have devastating consequences. The Salem witch trials is one of history's most famous examples. In the late 1600s, accusations of witchcraft began running through a small Massachusetts village. By the time it was over, one hundred fifty people had been accused and jailed.

Nineteen of them were ultimately executed because no one was willing to step up and challenge the group. The failure of the *Challenger* disaster in 1986 has largely been attributed to herd thinking; scientists knew there was the potential for fault in the shuttle's O-rings when the temperature dropped below a certain level, but groupthink prevented those concerns from being heard. More recently, cancel culture, the online affinity to culturally block a popular figure because of a perceived offense, has also taken hold. We must all recognize when we are part of these behaviors, intentionally or unintentionally.

When a human lighthouse sees you in the midst of your storm, it points you toward safety and protection. In doing so, it also sends you an uncompromising message of belief: Yes, the situation is difficult, but you are not alone. I'm standing right here with you, and I know the way home.

I can still remember the final day I walked up the steps of that abusive foster home with my social worker, Mike Silvia. A violent confrontation had unfolded that cold December morning, and I had fled the house and headed for Mike's office. An argument ensued between him and my foster parents, and they finally agreed to release me from their custody. Mike and I returned to the home to get my belongings, both of us bracing for what was certainly going to be a confrontation. I vividly recall standing shoulder to shoulder with him and him nodding ever so slightly at me, as if to say, "Whatever is on the other side of that door, we are going to face it together." We all need someone to come stand by us from time to time. And we can also stand beside another, to answer their call for support in a time of need.

Many years after we first met, this was the kind of call I had to make to my uncle Greg.

There have always been questions in the Pemberton family as to whether my father, Kenny, knew of my existence. The reasoning was that had he known, there is simply no way he would have abandoned me. As one of the top amateur fighters in the country, he was respected and feared. Still, he had a soft spot for children, and having a child, even if unexpected, would have required him to step forward to take responsibility.

The problem was that this did not mesh with the facts as I came to learn them. My mother had not only identified Kenny as my father to her own family but had told him as well. Two people who knew of their relationship, including one who witnessed the conversation between my parents about my pending arrival, told me that Kenny initially denied paternity, though he knew it was at least possible, given their relationship. A friend of Kenny's shared with me before his passing that he had gone to visit Kenny one time and found him taking care of a young boy, whom he remembered as me, in large part because my blue eyes did not match Kenny's deep brown ones. When he questioned Kenny about this, he had responded simply by saying, "This is my son." I appreciated the story, but I also knew it would be virtually impossible to prove.

I understood that Kenny's absence in my life was not

how his family wanted to remember him. But the question of his responsibility was a secondary matter to me. For years I had walked through the world with the weight of not knowing where I had come from. Finding my biological family had allowed me to finally put that burden down. Besides, I thought both could be true: that my father had many extraordinary qualities *and* he did not make the best decisions when it came to my sudden arrival in the world. Over time, and with the wisdom gained from my own lighthouses, I saw his lack of responsibility as a reflection of his own difficult childhood and the fact that he was twenty-one years old when I was born.

When I met the Pemberton family, I could see the resemblance between us, and so could they; it was very clear that I was a Pemberton and Kenny's son. They said as much, and so did their eyes. It was a look of recognition. When I petitioned a family court to change my last name from my birth name of Klakowicz to Pemberton, the Pemberton family did not protest.

Until one day, one of them did exactly that.

One of Greg's brothers decided nearly thirty years later that I was not a Pemberton after all. He penned a self-published, incoherent pamphlet, basing the title off my book, accusing me of making up the story of my early years and emphatically denying that Kenny Pemberton was my father. He offered no evidence for his claims about my childhood other than an uninformed speculative opinion. On the other hand, I had my case file, spanning twenty-five years, along with many hours of recorded interviews with Kenny's family and friends as well as public records.

In essence, I did not write anything I could not prove or defend.

I can't say this broadside surprised me. I had been warned over and over again by his siblings and Kenny's friends that this particular family member was capable of this behavior. Over the years, I had followed their advice and kept my distance from him as a result.

Still, the allegation that I was not a Pemberton was far more serious, especially when he took to asserting that another man was my father, going so far as to include the deceased man's photo in his booklet. That was followed by a lengthy social media campaign selling his pamphlet, asserting time and time again that I had been untruthful. It was readily apparent that his only motivation was to sow seeds of doubt, an effort that was destined to fail.

My first thought was my children. I sat down with them to explain the situation and most important of all convey that Pemberton was indeed their last name, that I would never have allowed them to walk through the world with a name that was not theirs. I then called Uncle Greg to tell him what had unfolded. He was furious and frustrated, unable to understand why his brother had taken this route, especially nearly three decades after my initial meetings with the Pembertons. When I asked Greg to take a familial DNA test with me to prove scientifically what the Pembertons had told me years ago, he readily agreed. As we awaited the results, I remarked that if the DNA test showed we were not related, I was going to adopt him as my uncle in any event. When the test came back with 99.8 percent accuracy, we shared a long hug.

Greg understood the impact of having someone try to rip away the identity I had spent so long trying to find. He understood perhaps better than most what a long search for family felt like, the rootlessness an orphan feels, the desire for connection they seek, and their restlessness until they find it. He also understood the importance of finding the truth wherever it might lead. It meant a great deal that he would stand by me in a time when I needed support. Greg's uncompromising belief is not only about his own worth and value but about mine as well.

CHAPTER 5

RICK ROCK

If there is any immortality to be had in
us human beings, it is certainly only to
be found in the love we leave behind.
Fathers like mine don't ever die.
—LEO BUSCAGLIA

E very Father's Day you'll find me on the golf course,
playing in the early hours of the morning before my
family wakes up. I discovered the game when I was thirty
years old, the sanctity and the quiet, the competition and
the camaraderie all speaking to me. Out on the course,
among my closest friends and in the peace of nature, life
slows down.

Walking the course with me on those special Sundays
for the last several years has been Dr. Rick Rock. We met
a few years ago when he walked over to introduce himself

before a round. We hit it off immediately. You won't spend too much time with Rick before you realize that his great passions are his family, golf, medicine, and Marquette University, where he attended.

This particular Father's Day could not have been better. The temperature was perfect and there was no wind to speak of, a rarity in the Chicagoland area. Doc Rock, as he is sometimes called, is always noticeable from a few holes away because he has a shock of white hair peeking out from under his golf cap. Rick's golf ball always moves from right to left; it is so consistent that you don't even need to look to see where it lands. As he teed off on the next-to-last hole, the ball taking its familiar trajectory, I couldn't resist the opportunity to tease him. "Just one time I want to see you hit the ball from left to right," I remarked, "you know, slice it like the rest of us do."

"Can't do it," he said, smiling.

We walked down the fairway, enjoying the quiet of the morning and lost in our own thoughts. As we approached Rick's ball, sitting perfectly in the fairway, I turned to say "nice shot," but as I did, I could see his face flushed with emotion.

"Doc, you okay?"

"I am," he replied, quietly. "Just thinking about my dad."

I nodded in understanding. Throughout the morning, I had been quietly thinking about my father as well. Father's Day is a day to reflect on the fathers we are and the fathers we came from. But for Rick, Father's Day carries an additional significance because it was on this day at the age of sixteen that his life changed dramatically.

Rick's immediate family, as well as his extended family, had come from Budapest, Hungary, fleeing the country's growing communist movement. Rick's grandfather was a blacksmith in Hungary, and his grandmother was a cook for a Russian duke. In America, his grandfather became a tool-and-die man at International Harvester, and his grandmother cooked for families in St. Stephen's Parish, a large Hungarian community in Roseland, Illinois.

The family surname was Rakaczky but was shortened to Rock upon their arrival in their new land. Motivated by the family's desire to succeed in America, Rick's father, Robert, was focused on education, ultimately attending dental school and obtaining a residency in oral surgery at Cook County Hospital. But soon he heard the call of country and enlisted to serve in the Korean War. When he went to enlist, he had an elevated heart rate, and they refused him. He took the needed medication to slow his heart rate and returned, reapplying for service. He served four years in the Korean War on a battleship where the majority of his time was spent reconstructing the faces of those who had been seriously wounded. While in Korea he contracted malaria, and the lingering effects would impact his health for the rest of his life.

Robert Rock came back from Korea and returned to his practice as a dentist. He fell in love with and married Marjorie Diesel, a young woman from Lockport, Illinois. They adopted their first child, Robert Rock Jr., believing they couldn't have biological children. Shortly after the adoption, as often happens, there was a surprise pregnancy. Rick's brother John was born, followed by Rick two years later, and a younger brother, Bill, arriving five years after Rick. Initially, the Rocks lived in a modest apartment above the dental practice. But as the practice expanded, they built a home outside Lockport, Illinois, living a comfortable middle-class existence. In many ways, the Rocks were the epitome of the American dream.

Father's Day Weekend in 1969 saw the family of six heading in different directions, with an agreement to celebrate the day a bit later. Rick and his dad headed to the family farm in Wisconsin. His dad purchased the farm because it reminded him of his early childhood in Hungary. On weekends, he would often go to the family farm to check on the house and work the land.

The morning of Father's Day, Rick could tell his father wasn't feeling well. He called a local doctor, who prescribed nitroglycerin. After hanging up the phone, Rick's dad turned to him and said, "I'm not feeling that well. I think we should go home. I'll lie down for a while; you go ahead and take a shower and pack. You have your license now and can drive us back." When Rick emerged from the shower, he heard loud gasps coming from his father's bedroom. He ran to his father's room to see him in the throes of a massive heart attack. Unaware of what to do, Rick watched helplessly as his father took his last breaths. Now alone, he walked to the kitchen to call home to tell his family what had happened. No one answered. Finally, he was able to reach Father Adams, who like his dad had grown up in Hungary. Father Adams drove to the church where Rick's mom and brothers were attending mass and broke the news that Dr. Rock had suddenly passed away.

Rick folds his hands quietly as he tells the story of losing his dad on Father's Day when Rick was just sixteen. "What I remember more than anything else were his last breaths and the overwhelming feeling of not being able to help him."

Not only had the family lost their patriarch, but the family's entire way of life changed. Though a successful practicing dentist, Dr. Rock didn't have much life insurance or a pension for the family to draw on. His mother sat her sons down and told them that with their dad gone, they would all have to adjust their lives and take on greater responsibility in the family. Rick began working odd jobs, from laying blacktop to making baby powder, to help his mother and to continue to attend his private school.

Rick had lost his guide at a time when he most needed him. But others would step in to try to fill the void. Pat Sullivan, his high school basketball and soccer coach, and Matt Senffner, his baseball and football coach, took Rick under their wing. They became guides, giving Rick direction and support when needed. Rick also discovered a new strength in his mother, especially when budget cuts threatened to close down his school. She became a major fundraising force behind the effort that successfully kept the doors of Providence Catholic High School open. Less than two years after his dad's passing, Rick graduated as the school's salutatorian and received the Scholar-Athlete Award.

Rick had always excelled in math and had considered becoming a math teacher or perhaps an engineer. But that changed when his father passed away. He wanted to know what should have been done and what *he* could have done to save his father. And medicine would be able to provide those answers. Never again, he thought, was he going to be without solutions.

When the time came to apply to college, Rick's first choice was Marquette University. Marquette had offered him a partial scholarship to play soccer and join his brother John, who was the goalkeeper for the team. The money he had saved from summer jobs and his dad's social security benefits helped fill in the remaining gaps. He excelled at Marquette as a premed major and as a star soccer player, winning the school's McCahill Award, presented to the senior athlete who has demonstrated the highest performance in scholarship, leadership, and athletics. Soon he set his sights on medicine and the prestigious university of health sciences—Chicago Medical School.

The odds were daunting; there were 10,000 applications for 150 spots. Some people pursue a career in medicine because they had parents who were doctors and want to carry on the family tradition. Others' primary motivation is the money or the prestige. But Rick had remembered something his dad had said while they worked the land on the farm in Wisconsin: "I chose medicine because I wanted to take care of people."

Rick gained admission to the famed medical school, the last three-year program to run in the United States. He began his medical school classes three weeks after he graduated from Marquette. When he arrived, he knew no one and felt in the minority in a predominately Jewish medical school. But the aspiring physicians learned pretty quickly that the only way they could get through the rigorous demands of medical school was if they bonded together.

Rick chose obstetrics and gynecology as his focus. It is a particularly demanding aspect of medicine; life enters our world on its own timetable. Rick loved it immediately. It allowed him to be immersed in the world of medicine, perform surgery, and form lifelong relationships.

Rick graduated and started his medical practice. One New Year's Day while home, Rick received an urgent call. One of his patients had begun having complications with her pregnancy. He had already admitted her to the hospital and placed her on bed rest and was monitoring her progress closely, hoping she could get to full-term so the baby might have the best chance at survival. But at two o'clock in the morning on New Year's Day, her condition worsened severely. Rick raced to the hospital and performed an emergency C-section. The baby was healthy, but now the mother was in great danger; she had continued to hemorrhage after the delivery. Two hours later, Rick had to perform an emergency hysterectomy to try to save her life.

In the middle of that procedure, the first-time mom suffered a pulmonary embolism. Pulmonary embolisms, or PEs as they are referred to by doctors, are incredibly dangerous. Originating somewhere in the body, these blood clots then travel to the lungs, cutting off oxygen. Further complicating matters, the hospital was short-staffed. The anesthesiologist who had joined Rick in the operating room had to call in a third doctor to help because of the complexity of the mom's condition. The three doctors worked furiously to save her, exchanging anxious glances at the first sign of a drop in her blood pressure. Finally, after several long hours, she began to stabilize.

That case was the most complicated—and the most challenging—of Rick's storied career in medicine. Later on, he would read studies on similar cases and learn that the woman had only a 2 percent chance of survival. But he didn't know that at the time, nor would he have cared.

"There was no time to be nervous or afraid," he told me one time while we grabbed a beer after a round of golf. "All I cared about was saving her life. I knew I had to do all I could, to call on every professional skill and personal experience I had. Two days later the emotional impact of it all hit me. What if I had lost her? I already knew the impact this would have on her family and the daughter who would never meet her mom. I *had* to save her."

He leaned forward, his bright blue eyes taking on heightened intensity. "Medicine is a competitive challenge. Either you win or you lose, especially when you are performing surgeries or delivering babies. And you don't want to lose in medicine. You have to win. It is you against the disease, you against the disruption, with a life hanging in the balance."

Still, there are times when the outcome is not what he fought for. In those instances, he is taken back to that fateful Father's Day morning that changed everything. Today Rick has his wife, Buffy, of nearly four decades to remind him that now, as it was then, he did everything he possibly could.

Rick had been raised in a faith-abiding household, and prayer has been a staple throughout his life, from his medical school days and into medical practice. He has asked God to give him the wisdom to heal a life or bring another into the world, to help him make the right decisions, to be strong and to accept when he has given his best. Never were his prayers more fervent than at two o'clock in the morning when he was summoned to the bedside of a patient in critical condition, her life hanging in the balance.

On occasion, Dr. Rock hears the whisper of retirement, but he has yet to listen to its voice. Though he no longer delivers babies, the healing element that medicine provides still drives Rick. Now his focus is on treating women going through menopause, a tremendous shock and trauma to their system. Waves of hot flashes are often accompanied by feelings of sadness and anxiety that appear without warning. There is no way of knowing how long menopause will last; it can be months or years before the symptoms subside. For many women, they lose their sense of self, held hostage by an invisible force that comes and goes as it pleases.

Many of Rick's patients initially come to him feeling as if they have a dark cloud over their head. They are often told their only choice is antidepressants. And yet the research shows that by restoring their hormones into balance and integrating proper diet and exercise, along with positive reinforcement from their family, most women can have the quality of life they deserve. Rick loves hearing from his patients, like the woman who recently called, her voice filled with emotion: "I cannot believe how different I feel. You have changed my life." It is the patients who once felt hopeless, and who later have their hope restored, that motivate Rick to keep helping and healing.

Fatherhood has brought its own kind of healing. Few people I know enjoy their children as much as Rick Rock enjoys his three daughters, Maddie, Margee, and Kathleen.

He has always been present in their lives, doting on them as dads with daughters often do, helping them realize their own individual talents and gifts. He asks of himself all the questions that conscientious dads do: "Am I a good dad? Have I done all the right things?" He is his daughters' superhero and they, along with the ever-devoted Buffy, are his greatest joy. I often receive updates on the family and the career pursuits and relationships of his daughters; it is a running joke between us that the boyfriends have to meet Uncle Steve before they get approval.

Men who lose their fathers at an early age carry two numbers with them—their current age and the age their father died. This reluctant fraternity live in fear that they will die sooner or at the same age, as if a generational curse might be lurking, just waiting to strike. When they pass that grim milestone, they breathe a sigh of relief. And then they count the years that they have lived longer, grateful that they have lasted long enough to become a father and grandfather, trying to live the life their father was denied.

So it is with Dr. Rick Rock. His father's life is still his lighthouse. As time and life move on, and now as a father, Rick is ever mindful of the man his dad was, his lessons of discipline, service, and education firmly imprinted. And those lessons show up in the way Rick heals.

The Lighthouse Effect: Helping and Healing

Human lighthouses bend the arc of our lives. They appear to us as real-life angels. And they are. But there is no such thing as a pristine lighthouse, unmarked by the elements of the sea. From a distance the lighthouse is majestic and magnificent, but as you get closer, you'll see that the lighthouse is windswept and weathered. It pays a price for the mission it fulfills. We are so appreciative of their kindness that we might not notice that lighthouses often guide us from a place of loss themselves. Part of their motivation for being a lighthouse is because they remember their own storms and the times they needed lighthouses.

When life storms batter us, we often try to find some way to repair ourselves, to put the pain down or aside. What we are seeking is healing. That healing can come from our faith, our family, and our friends. Or it can come simply with the passage of time. But it can also come from shifting our own struggle toward that which might better the lives of others, to turn our pain into someone else's possibility. Perhaps in providing another with what we needed most, we continue to find a path to healing ourselves.

Healing Hands

The loss of Dr. Robert Rock was a tragedy that unfolded without warning, and it so quickly altered the family that they barely had time to mourn his passing. Yet there is a direct connection between Rick losing his father and the life of healing he chose: the man who once watched helplessly as his guide and mentor took his last breath has helped many others take their first.

> Providing another with what you needed most is the path to healing yourself.

If you live this life and breathe this air, you will encounter adversity. You may wish that weren't the case, but there are no smooth seas in life. You try to protect yourself and your loved ones as best you can, but there are no guarantees. Still, these challenges take their toll; some days you struggle to put both feet on the floor. A tragedy, a long-standing friendship that dissolves, a family dispute, or the sudden loss of a job can all leave you with a gap in your life. Events can seem out of your control, and you can feel incredibly helpless, struggling to move on. Even when you do, the memories of a difficult time are still with you. But life does move on—with or without your acceptance. The question now is in which direction will it move—and for whom?

The helplessness and vulnerability Rick felt that June morning long ago allow him to assist his patients today at critical junctures in their lives. This might be the case for you too. Perhaps the pain of your past is a present reality for someone else. When others see that you have made it through, it gives them hope that they can find a path through their own struggles.

Turning Trials into Trajectory

After the loss of his father, Rick Rock focused on what he still had: his mother and brothers, his church, his high school coaches, and then later on his cherished Marquette University. The path to healing can be extraordinarily long and difficult, but we *do* have the ability to begin again. Focusing on what we still have, as opposed to that which is no longer, is a first step to turning trials into trajectory.

Many of us have examples in our lives of the proof of this approach, though the circumstances might not be as severe as what Rick faced. You had something that didn't quite work out the way you planned: a relation-ship, a job, or a business you started. At the time, the setback was distress-ing and upsetting. You

> Starting over may be long and difficult, but you *do* have the ability to begin again.

wondered what you were going to do next. But those trials became the foundation for a new direction. You learned something from that hardship, and you applied it the next time around. Soon you experienced little successes: You went out on a blind date or had a promising job interview. A friend approached you with a new business idea.

These experiences begin to restore our sense of purpose, and as more time passes, we arrive at a place in our lives where we begin to take flight again. Now when we look back at those situations that did not unfold the way we planned, we have a completely different view of those disappointments. We not only feel differently about them but are grateful they did not work out the way we wanted them to. Why? Because we now realize that the struggle, though we did not like it, brought us to a place of meaning again.

But turning trials into trajectory is not just about us. It also applies to the impact we can have on others. You see this in Rick's life: High school coaches surrounded him with support, and he found meaning in working odd jobs to help support the family. In medical school, he developed a camaraderie with his classmates who were taking on the same challenge that he was. Those moments, while they couldn't replace what was lost, still mattered.

Take Your Own Temperature

There is ample opportunity for us to look around the world and see the great need for healing. This is particularly true in light of the devastation of COVID-19 on our lives, our families, and our economy. As we find normalcy again, we will have to be actively engaged in the process of healing. But that process must first start with our own healing.

That begins with taking your own temperature, deliberately considering the things in your life that you would like to repair or restore. This could be a family relationship, a tense exchange with a coworker, or a disagreement with a friend that has not been resolved. You may have to extend the olive branch or offer forgiveness to bring the situation to closure. But taking that step will relieve you of any unsettled feelings and provide the chance to build something new—and better.

Healing also means addition by subtraction: letting go of old disputes, or stepping away from toxic relationships or experiences. This also applies to the negative stories you might have told yourself about your talents or your value. Health is about not only what we feed our bodies but also what we feed our minds. Be attentive to the whispers of pessimism, and replace them with voices of assurance and support.

Several years ago, Dr. Rick Rock was dining at a restaurant with one of his daughters when a woman and a little girl nervously approached his table.

"I'm sorry to interrupt you, but I wanted to come over and say hello. Do you remember me?" she asked. This was a common occurrence for Dr. Rock, who over the course of his thirty-year career has delivered over four thousand children. Ordinarily, he has to search his memory to recall the patient. But that wasn't necessary this time.

"I certainly do," he replied.

Turning to her daughter, the woman said, "This is Dr. Rick Rock, the man who saved my life. I'm here with you today because of him. He knew just what to do."

CHAPTER 6

CARMEN ORTIZ-MCGHEE

*One day you will tell your story of
how you overcame what you're going
through now and it will become part
of someone else's survival guide.*

—JOHBAG MNOLA

My favorite means of transportation is the train, specifically the Acela Express that rumbles up and down the Eastern Seaboard of the United States. There are no long security lines, multiple checkpoint screenings, or stops to fill up the gas tank. You simply put your bag in the overhead bin, grab a comfortable seat, and let someone else do the driving. Cell phone service can be spotty, a wonderful inconvenience that allows for some much-needed quiet time in an overscheduled world.

Perhaps the best part of the experience are the many

communities the train pulls through, from Penn Station's hustling and bustling underground in New York City, to New London, Connecticut's seaport station that runs alongside the Atlantic Ocean. There is a beautiful diversity of life and the way people live it. I always take a window seat to witness this unfolding of humanity as people, wearing their respective uniforms of backpacks and business attire, exit and depart toward lives unknown. I took the train even more frequently while I was writing *A Chance in the World*. Headphones in with quiet jazz playing, I could block out the world and write, the only interruption a stolen glance out the window or the monotone announcement of our next stop.

On one particular trip, a familiar face interrupted my train ritual. Bespectacled and quick to laugh, Joe Watson and I had crossed paths several times because of our mutual work in the world of corporate recruiting. Joe was then chairman of the nonprofit Marathon Club, an organization involved with investment capital. We had also done some work together at Monster.com, where I worked as a senior executive. Joe was also an author, and I had reached out to him about my book. We exchanged a few pleasantries as the train bumped and rattled out of Penn Station.

"Hey," he said, "why don't you come back and sit with me? I'm sitting with the president of the Marathon Club. We have an open seat at our table."

I joined him a few moments later and introduced myself to Carmen Ortiz-McGhee. Warm and engaging, she had a wonderful smile that reached her eyes. The three of us talked about our respective careers and our families, and Joe kept us laughing with stories of his travel adventures.

After a few more minutes of conversation, Joe announced his departure. "I have a ticket upgrade to first class, and since you two are getting along so well, I'm going to leave you two to connect."

"You know, Joe," I offered, "if I didn't know you better, I'd think you deliberately asked me to sit here so you wouldn't leave Carmen alone and you could go hang out with the upper-class folks." Carmen laughed in agreement.

Joe put up his hands in a you-got-me gesture. "Guilty as charged, Your Honor."

"So, Steve," Carmen said pleasantly after Joe had made his way down the aisle of the train. "Joe mentioned you're writing a book. What's it about?"

For the next few minutes, I gave her the cruising altitude version: after I graduated from college I went searching for my biological family and managed to find them. It was a story I wanted to write for my young children who had begun asking me about my early years. For a time we talked about our families, and it wasn't hard to see that her husband and her three children were the center of her universe.

Soon, though, the subject returned to my writing. She was naturally curious and had quite a few questions about the process of writing a book.

"It sounds like you're thinking about a book yourself," I noted. "They say everybody has a book in them."

"Maybe one day," she replied. "It seems like such a big undertaking."

"It is, to be honest," I responded. "It's a real act of discipline. But absolutely possible."

"Have you ever gotten writer's block?" she asked. In the

background, the conductor announced Philadelphia as our next stop.

"Not yet," I replied, "but what I am experiencing is something else. I want to write about a topic with a certain level of depth, but I can't because I haven't experienced it. In my case, it's the subject of parents. I never knew mine, and the foster homes I was raised in . . . well, let's say they didn't fit the bill. I just don't know what it's like to have parents. Something that is so universal to everyone else is so foreign to me. Does that make any sense?"

"It does," she said quietly, looking out the window. Her reflection showed in the glass as the outside world whipped past. "A bit more than you know."

For the remainder of our train ride to Washington, DC, I sat and listened as Carmen shared a chapter of her own story.

Carmen's mother-in-law believes in family. That was a large part of the reason she pestered her daughter-in-law to try to locate her father. Carmen insisted it wasn't necessary. Then in her midtwenties, she had been without a father for so long, it no longer seemed unusual. Besides, he was not the kind of man she *wanted* to know. He had been briefly married to her mom, but the marriage ended quickly when it became clear he was an abusive man.

Married shortly after college, Carmen and her husband, Frank, had three children in the span of four years. As the children grew older, her mother-in-law's nudging intensified. "You should find out for health reasons, for the children's sake." In addition, Carmen's father-in-law had passed away a year after Carmen and Frank married. "If the children have a grandfather out there, they should at least meet him. Don't rob them of the chance to have a grandfather."

Carmen knew her mother-in-law was right, but still she had reservations. *What if he is the same kind of person he was? What if he doesn't want to be contacted?* Ultimately, the need to know for her children's sake overruled her concerns. She knew a few details about him: he was Mexican, his first name was William, and he had served in the military.

She knew she needed more information to begin her search and called her mom one night after the children had gone to bed, explaining that she was trying to gather more information about her father.

"Mom, did you say his people were from New Mexico or Arizona?" Carmen asked.

There was a lengthy silence and then a long sigh. "Carmen, let's catch up about this tomorrow. There are some things we need to discuss."

Every family has secrets. And some things are best left undiscussed. Unbeknownst to Carmen, there had been a lifelong secret between her and her mom: the identity of Carmen's father.

They met the following morning. Her mother paused for a moment as if gathering her strength. "I knew one day you would want to know more about your father. And it looks like that day is today." She paused again, as she often does when she wants to say something important.

"This man William you are asking about. He is not your father. Do you remember the stories I used to tell you about a man named Andy?"

Carmen nodded. "Your face would always light up when you talked about him."

"Well," she paused, taking a deep breath. "He is your father."

Magda Ortiz, Carmen's mother, grew up in a tight-knit, Catholic, Puerto Rican military family. Her father had served in the United States Army for thirty-one years and in three wars—World War II, Korea, and Vietnam. For several years the family was stationed in Munich, Germany. It was there that Magda attended the University of Maryland's Munich campus. One night while at the movies with friends, she met a handsome young man named Julio Angel Paerez, whose nickname was Andy. A whirlwind romance unfolded.

Andy was in the military, but it wasn't easy for him. At nineteen years old, he struggled with authority and found the rigid discipline of the army difficult, a situation that was not helped by cultural and language barriers. At his earliest opportunity, he decided he would go back to his native Puerto Rico.

But there was a development of which Andy was unaware: he was going to be a father. The news was not well-received by Magda's parents. Not only was their daughter having a child out of wedlock, but the father was someone who was not college educated, rebelled against authority in general, and had left the military. In their view, he was not worthy of their daughter.

For a Catholic Puerto Rican family steeped in military service, the circumstances of Carmen's arrival in the early 1970s would not only raise eyebrows but would also require some explanation. Magda's mother did not relish facing the judgment of her husband's family. They had always believed she thought she was better than them because of her privileged upbringing, so she decided to invent a story explaining her daughter's pregnancy: Magda had been married, but the marriage lasted for only two years before they divorced. For nearly thirty years, this story would stick, until Carmen, now a mother herself, began asking about her father's whereabouts.

Once Andy arrived back in Puerto Rico, Magda shared the news that he was going to be a father. He was surprised and overjoyed. Still very much in love and now bonded by having created a life together, Andy and Magda stayed in touch for the first year of Carmen's life. Letters and baby pictures were mailed back and forth across the Atlantic. Then the unthinkable happened.

Carmen's maternal grandmother and paternal grandmother, believing they were protecting their children, intercepted Andy's and Magda's letters, eventually cutting the would-be lovers off from each other. They each believed their beloved had lost interest and no longer cared. Andy went forward with his life, eventually marrying and having two daughters.

Magda married as well, when Carmen was two, but the marriage to William lasted only six months. This was the man Carmen had been raised to believe was her father. When the marriage ended, Magda became a single parent.

Magda and Carmen stayed in Germany with her grand-parents for five more years. Continuing a tradition of service to country, Magda pursued a career in military intelligence, one of the first Hispanic women to do so. It was a journey that would eventually bring her and her young daughter to Virginia.

For most of her life, Carmen didn't miss having a father. Her mother made sure she never felt unloved or abandoned. Once Carmen had been told the story of her father, she never questioned it. Since she didn't have any memories of him, there was no real connection to the idea of a father.

After high school Carmen went off to the University of Virginia, where she met the man who would one day be her husband. She graduated from college, married him two years later, and they immediately started having children.

Carmen settled into life as a wife and mother. In her professional life, she climbed through the world of nonprofit executive leadership, advocating on behalf of minority-owned financial services firms. A CEO by thirty-three, she was every bit a trailblazer as a Latina woman in that pro-fession as her mother had been in military intelligence. Life had settled into a routine—until a persistent mother-in-law and an early-morning conversation brought new develop-ments into her life.

In January 2004, Carmen started a new job. One of her first responsibilities was to help plan and coordinate a major conference taking place in June in Puerto Rico. For the next six months, she worked hard to impress her new colleagues and her boss. A week before the conference, she and the team met with a historian who was going to provide a history of Puerto Rico for the conference attendees.

They had lunch with the historian, listening in rapt attention as he walked through the history of the island. In the course of the presentation, he mentioned a number of towns, including San Lorenzo, where Andy was born.

After the presentation, Carmen pulled aside her boss and dear friend, who was born and raised in Puerto Rico. "He mentioned San Lorenzo. That's where my father is from."

She asked, "What's your father's name?

"Julio Paerez."

Her friend spoke in a rapid-fire manner and with a beautifully accented dialect: "Aye, Carmen, you use the superpagespr.com and look up the name Paerez, because you know Paerez is an unusual name, and you know it is a small town. And if there is one Paerez, he is related to another Paerez, so it's probably going to be family anyway."

Carmen wasn't sure it would be that easy, but when she returned to her office, her curiosity got the better of her. She went to superpagespr.com, and the first name in her search results was Julio A. Paerez. Two hours later, when her work was done, she got in her car and immediately called the number from the super pages.

A mean, rude voice growled, "Hello." This was the sound of someone who did not like being disturbed.

She hesitated. *How do you begin this kind of conversation? What if he doesn't want to hear from me? It's been thirty years.*

"Hi," she said cautiously. "Is Julio Paerez there?"

"No."

"Does he live there?"

"No."

"Do you know him?"

"Yes."

This is what I feared. If I tell him who I am, he's going to hang up. Thinking quickly, she made up a story. "My name is Carmen. I'm doing some research for my grandfather who used to coach a baseball team in the army. He wants to have a reunion of all the Puerto Rican players from his team. I'm just doing the research, so could you give him a message?"

"Yes—give me your number, and I'll pass it on."

Carmen gave the gruff voice her number. Twenty minutes later, a young woman—a teenager—called back. "Who are you? Why are you calling? What do you want?"

Carmen felt like she was being interrogated. Again, Carmen repeated the baseball reunion story.

"Hmm." The wordless response was purposefully long to let Carmen know she did not believe her. "Okay, well I'll just pass the message along."

Forty minutes passed, and Carmen got a call from another gentleman, this one far kinder and more hesitant than the first. She was anxious and so nervous that she repeated the fake story.

He answered slowly, quietly. "Well . . . I never played baseball."

Carmen felt rejected. He had to know who she was. She had introduced herself as Carmen, and he knew he had a daughter named Carmen. Masking her disappointment, Carmen said, "Oh, thank you. I'm sorry for bothering you."

She quickly hung up. Her feeling that her father did not want to hear from her had been realized.

But at her core, Carmen is a fighter, and she summoned that fighting spirit in that moment: *You may not want a relationship with me, but there is no way I'm going to let you deny me.*

She called back. "Listen, I wasn't exactly forthcoming with you the last time I called. I am Carmen Ortiz, and I am looking for my father. I think you are him. I won't bother you after this call. I just want to know if it is true."

"Yes," her father replied, followed by a brief silence. "I didn't say yes before because I didn't know what you knew. I thought your grandfather might be using you to find me to confront me. I didn't want to hurt you. But, yes, I am your father."

For Carmen, this reunion felt odd. She had long believed that the absence of a father had not mattered; now she found herself struggling to find the right words to express what she was feeling. "I'm not asking you for anything . . . I have been extraordinarily blessed in my life and career . . . I am happily married with three kids . . ." She rambled on, caught between the worlds of reaching out and explaining to a man she had never met. "I just want to meet you. I'm going to be in Puerto Rico next week. Would you be willing to meet me?"

He answered immediately, "Yes, absolutely. Just tell me where to be." Then he asked, "Your mom, how is she doing?"

A week later in Puerto Rico, Carmen was working hard to impress in her new role. The conference brought together some of the most accomplished and influential Latinos in the world, and Carmen's boss expected perfection. The success of the event was crucial for her and her organization. Carmen had confidence in her ability and in her team. She was less certain about the other matter that was causing her anxiety: meeting her father for the first time.

The plan had been set in motion. They were to meet at 8:00 p.m. in the lobby of the Ritz Carlton in San Juan, where her event was being held. The evening of their meeting, Carmen was a blur of activity, making calls and finalizing details for the conference.

On the phone with the convention chair, Carmen spotted her father immediately. He was with another man, about his age, and they were quite obviously not Ritz Carlton patrons, given their dress and demeanor. He had two bundles of roses in one arm and another small package in the other. He was clearly nervous and shaking so much that he had to put the bundles down in the chair next to him. As he scanned the room of people bustling about, he smiled at Carmen in a cordial greeting, and she smiled back. He clearly didn't realize who she was, expecting his long-lost daughter to look more like her mother.

She completed her call and walked straight up to him. "Are you Julio Paerez?"

He took one look at Carmen and scooped her up in a massive bear hug. He squeezed hard and didn't let go. His emotions overcame him and he sobbed deeply, trying to speak but each time overcome with more emotion. She was shocked and surprised at his reaction, and in that moment, she realized this meeting meant everything to him. For her part, she felt relief that he was glad to see her. She was happy that he was happy. Yet for reasons she couldn't fully understand, the magnitude of the moment did not fully hit her.

Carmen invited him to the pool where she had a surprise for him: her mother and daughter had joined her on the trip. For the first time in thirty years, Andy and Magda laid eyes on each other.

Carmen soon discovered that the young girl who had called her back was her baby sister, who had always known about her older sister. After she spoke to Carmen, she called their father, saying, "I think your daughter is looking for you."

He had responded, "You're wrong. She is not looking for me. It's been thirty years."

In true Puerto Rican form, her new sister said, "Listen, if that is my sister and you don't call her and I don't get to meet her, then I will call her and figure out who she is."

Her father also admitted he had come with a friend that day for moral support, not knowing how Carmen would react. The friend was ready to support him if the meeting went south.

At the end of the weeklong conference, Andy came back to the hotel to get Carmen and her family. He picked them up—Carmen, along with her mom and daughter and several of Carmen's colleagues—and headed to the postcard-picture kiosks at Luquillo Beach. The kiosks were brightly decorated with varying shades of vivid colors. The smell of delectable Puerto Rican foods filled the air, and all around was the lively music of the island.

Carmen's father beamed and smiled the entire time and

was particularly fascinated by his granddaughter, Jordan. He doted on her, buying her trinkets and stuffed animals and letting her ride every dime pony along the kiosks.

He then turned his attention to Carmen. He headed to a jukebox and played a salsa song and extended his hand, asking Carmen to dance. Carmen hesitated. She had grown up culturally isolated in private Catholic schools in Northern Virginia, where Latinos were few and far between. But her mother, for whom *familia* is everything, made sure that Carmen felt connected to their Puerto Rican culture, whether it be through dancing, cooking, or music. It was salsa that particularly captured Carmen's heart so much that at one point, she had secret aspirations to pursue Latin dance as a profession. With its lively rhythms and resounding beat, salsa is an anchor of Puerto Rican culture.

Salsa had kept her connected to her people and her culture. Now, as Carmen looked at her long-lost father's extended hand, salsa was going to connect her to the man she thought she would never meet. As she danced with her father, the enormity of the moment finally hit her—what had been lost and what could still be. Emotions flooded her being, and now it was her turn to be overwhelmed, to hug him long and hard, unable to speak and unwilling to let go. Her mother and daughter looked on, overcome with tears of joy.

When they pulled apart, he pulled a ring from his finger and placed it on hers. Then he held out the other bundle he had brought the first day. In his excitement, he had forgotten to give it to her. She opened it and was greeted by a well-worn picture that had hung in his home for three decades. It was of her as a baby. Their eyes met, and then her father said the words that will forever remain with her.

"You see, my daughter, I have always loved you."

A couple of weeks prior to Carmen's dance with her father, I sat alone in the conference room of a television studio, staring at a small television screen. I was studying archived footage of a massive community protest in my hometown of New Bedford. That hot summer day in 1970, a Boston television station had come to the community, drawn by an interest in interviewing the residents.

As part of the research for my book, I wanted to gain an understanding of the tone of the times. I was also looking for something else: a glimpse of my father. At the time, he was one of the top amateur fighters in the world, and I'd already learned from newspaper accounts that he had been actively involved in bringing some calm to the city that had been aflame that summer. Perhaps, I reasoned, I might be able to see my father on camera or in the crowd.

Children who have never met their biological parents often long for some type of connection. They want to see the way they moved or talked, the way they smiled or walked so that they might be able to see themselves in another human being.

For nearly ninety minutes, grainy black-and-white images flickered across the screen. Residents flocked to the camera to share their anger at untenable employment conditions, and crowds assembled at city landmarks that I had seen growing up. As the tape neared its end, I stood up to stretch, concluding that my father was not in the footage.

The last segment of the footage showed yet another assembled crowd. A group of men had gathered to talk with the show's host to discuss the condition of the city and what should be done. One figure in the crowd with his back to the camera caught my eye because he was kneeling and shaking his head in quiet objection. Then he stood up and for a moment looked right into the camera and, it seemed, right at me. There was no mistaking who he was— the kneeling figure was my father. I paused the film to stare long and hard, and without realizing it, I touched the screen, once again trying to establish a connection with a father I never knew.

At the time of my chance meeting with Carmen, I was wrestling with the story of how I would write about my biological parents and their families. Like Carmen's, my story was filled with twists and turns. But those twists and turns would never bring me what I had long wished for: a chance to meet my mother and father. They had both passed away when I was a young boy, something I did not learn until years later. In hearing this joyful reunion of a father and daughter after thirty years, I was reminded of what I wished could have transpired for me. Had I been able to meet my mother or father, that is how I imagined it would have been. I smiled at the thought.

While I would come to learn the story of my parent's struggles, I had been primarily focused on what those struggles had cost me. I'd never really wrestled with how much their own losses and struggles had cost *them*. My father lost his mother to a sudden illness when he was just fourteen years old and the following week was placed in a juvenile home, not because he had done something wrong but because society didn't know what to do with him. In another part of the country, my mother was being raised by her mother while her father was fighting in World War II. But her mother was battling alcoholism and suffering a mental health crisis, creating an unstable household and a storm of its own. I had not fully appreciated these circumstances and the devastating impact they must have had on them. And because I hadn't, I had not truly forgiven them for what had unfolded in my childhood years. They were not bad people but had some bad things happen to them, things they were not equipped to handle.

Carmen had seen from the very beginning that well-intended forces in her parents' lives had kept them apart. She could have blamed her father for not working harder to seek her out all those years. But she understood what he was up against—a belief that her mother and her family did not want him in their lives. In the end, Carmen chooses the relationship she has with her father now, especially because she knows how much he always loved her.

Meeting her father also deepened Carmen's respect for her mother, who had lost a connection to a great love. Carmen had also fallen in love at the same age as her mom and could never imagine a world where the enormous love she has for her husband would be denied. She could have been upset with her mother for not telling her the truth earlier. But her mother had decided that she would tell her daughter the truth when she asked, in large part to protect her from any feeling of not being wanted. She hadn't imagined that the question would come much later in life.

Carmen has never felt disappointment over those lost years with her father. She came to understand the struggles of her mother and father—two young people in love who would be denied the opportunity to fully live that love for each other. But that love has endured in their daughter and their three grandchildren. Time has been lost, but not the future; that still remains in front of them.

The Lighthouse Effect: The First Picture Is Not the Full Story

In days of old, someone who cared for a lighthouse was called a lighthouse keeper. They lived in the lighthouse and had many responsibilities, from maintaining all the mechanical equipment to moving channel markers, the floating buoys that marked the safe boundaries within the channel. But there was no greater responsibility than to be on the lookout for ships in distress and to guide them to safety, especially in the midst of a storm.

In performing this most important duty, the lighthouse keeper also did something all lighthouses do without fail: *they do not pass judgment*. The lighthouse does not qualify your distress; it does not ask if you are black or white, wealthy or less so, Democrat or Republican. It does not concern itself with where you stand on a particular issue. Nor does it blame you for being in the middle of the storm.

Rather, its priority is how it might guide you toward safe harbor. The lighthouse knows you are more than its initial picture of you—that of the distressed traveler—and that you have a deeper, fuller story.

We are all flawed. We have all endured difficulties in our lives. When we recognize this, we can see the common threads that bind us: love and loss, disappointment and dreams, joy and pain. When we have been wronged or hurt, understanding our mutual chapters of tragedy and triumph can forge a path to forgiveness. This lesson from a stranger on a train on the importance of seeking the full story has stayed with me, though I suspect Carmen was unaware of its significance at the time. And it was not the last time I would learn something from her.

Meet People Where They Are

We all have pet peeves. One of mine: loud talkers on their cell phones. On trains (except the quiet car on the Acela!), in airports, at restaurants, in doctors' offices—they seem to be everywhere we turn. I have no particular reason for this reaction, other than mild frustration at the lack of manners. I quietly mutter to myself, "We get it! You are a very important person upon whom the entire fate of the universe rests."

The tone of these conversations, and the quick glances to make sure their offended audiences are listening, lets us know that some of this attention-seeking performance is born of a need to be seen or heard. But other issues may be unfolding in their lives: a divorce, a lack of confidence in their job, or feeling that they aren't valued in their personal relationships. Looking at attention-seeking behaviors—whether it be provocative social media posts or me-only conversations—through the lens of a deeper concern, provides us an opportunity to understand rather than judge. It also allows us to see that what we think is a flaw might be more of a coping mechanism to deal with a time of uncertainty.

Accepting people—and their behaviors—is one of the most important aspects of getting the full story. We can hope for people to be different, but when those wishes take up too much of our own mind space, it's time to let it go. It doesn't mean we don't draw boundaries (I walk away from the loud talkers). It doesn't mean we approve or condone the behavior, but it does mean we accept people as they are and not as we wish them to be. When Carmen found her dad, she accepted him as he was and not as she wished he could have been—and then chose to build a new beginning. Without it, she would not have the relationship she enjoys with him today.

You Needed Grace Once upon a Time

When we judge someone, that opinion falls into one of two areas, according to psychologists. In the first instance, we form an opinion based on what we think is their personality. For example, we've determined the person who just cut us off in traffic is an aggressive personality and drives that way all the time. In the second instance, our opinion about a person is based on something in their situation at that particular time. We believe the driver who cut us off might just be running late to work.

It is not hard to guess which of these judgments we often make: those focused on personality. It could be that it's simply easier to say, "I know exactly what this person is like because I've seen that personality before." What helps us navigate moments like these, and to show grace, is to remember a time when we needed understanding or empathy. We've all had bad days and tough moments, and in those moments what we needed was not to be judged but rather to be understood.

Judgment Is a Two-Way Street

We've all heard the many nuggets of wisdom about judgment:

> Judge not, lest ye be judged.
> Don't judge a book by its cover.
> Don't judge someone until you have walked a mile in
>   their shoes.

Beyond that wisdom, which many of us heard as children, we have also been on the receiving end of a bad opinion and should therefore know better than to judge. Still, we all pass judgment, in quiet ways and in other ways that are not so quiet. More recently, a different

> Remember a time when you needed understanding or empathy.

element has been added to our universe: social media. In that world, *everything* is open for opinion. The currency on which social media thrives is judgment. Within seconds, we can weigh in with our assessment of someone else, approvingly or disapprovingly, while offering opinions of our own.

This tendency does not make us bad people. It's simply human nature, our way of trying to organize the world that we are often too busy or impatient to understand. Henry David Thoreau said it well: "The question is not what you look at, but what you see."[1] And part of what we need to see is that passing judgment is often about something else: us.

We can try to dress up our judgment by saying we only want what's best for that person, even though we've not shared constructive feedback with them. We can assign it to the fact that we live in an overscheduled world and we don't have time to unpack people and their specific situations. But in the end, judgment says more about us than it does about the person on the receiving end.

Perhaps our need to judge comes because we feel uncertain, afraid, or envious or are stuck in our own lives. We may see others taking risks that we ourselves have not yet summoned the will to take. They may have achieved something we thought we could have—or should have—achieved. These are difficult reasons to admit, but the honesty is necessary. We should always try to refrain from quick judgment, but when we do judge someone, we should always take a closer look at our own motivations.

Get below the Waterline

Many of us often assess others by what we see: their gender, race, age, physical appearance, or accent. (On more than one occasion, strangers have rightly guessed that I grew up in

Massachusetts. My accent is a dead giveaway even though I can't hear it.) Some of these are attributes we come into the world with, and they are mostly things we cannot change, nor do we want to. They exist above the waterline, much like the tip of an iceberg. And like the iceberg, the labels we see are only the beginning of the story, not the end. They are our first picture but not the full story.

To see these physical characteristics makes us observant. But we get ourselves in difficulty when we assume we know someone's story because of what we initially see. *Everyone* has a story, and that story is rarely evident simply by looking at them. Yet we live in a world that continually sees the need

> **Everyone has a story that cannot be seen above the waterline.**

to render a verdict on our fellow human beings, as if the most important things we can ever learn about someone are those things above the waterline. These quick appraisals are routinely exploited by scheming advertisers, clickbait promoters, and disingenuous politicians who manipulate these tendencies for their own end. Much of the distrust and separation we see in our societies can be traced back to this behavior. Left unchecked, these snap judgments will be our undoing, and our well-intended attempts to unify, to find some common ground, will fall flat. Considering everyone we meet a "them" comes at immeasurable cost. The increasingly polarized world of the last several years shows us the price we pay.

There is a deeper, richer, and more unifying narrative. The full story of what unites us is to be found in the things we cannot see: in the music that moves us, the families we love, and the children we adore. Our more common story is to be found in the way we celebrate our culture or our faith, if we are the first in our family to go to college or have served our country. It can be uncovered when we learn that our grandparents were immigrants, or if we started a small business. As we get to know someone better, to learn their full story, we find that there are more things we have in common.

I learned this firsthand when I met my mother's family, the Murphys, and learned the story of my grandfather, Joseph Murphy. The son of Irish immigrants, he was born and raised in Philadelphia. In 1918 the flu pandemic descended on the city with great fury, killing twenty thousand people, including Joe's mother and father, both passing away within a week of each other.[2] Joe went to live with an uncle and his wife, who did not fully embrace young Joe. His childhood was turbulent and difficult, but he went on to serve the US in World War II, becoming highly decorated in the process. Later on he served as a technical writer for NASA. In Grandpa Joe's first picture, he would have appeared to be a spectacled, older white man who doted on his family. His fuller story was something more—an orphaned boy who became a war hero, a member of the Greatest Generation whose early years were eerily similar to mine.

As I neared completion of *A Chance in the World*, I asked several friends to take a look at the manuscript. I'd always appreciated Carmen's perspective and insights, and I wanted her thoughts on how I had captured the story of my parents, given her own experiences. She agreed to do so and was kind and gracious with her time and gave me wonderful feedback, along with a concluding note: "There is something else I want to share with you, but it's best done over the phone. It's about your sister. Give me a call when you get a chance."

When I discovered my biological family, I also learned for the first time that I was one of my mother's six children. The news came as quite a surprise; I had no memory of having brothers and sisters. My twin sister had passed away at birth, but amazingly, I managed to find and ultimately talk with my other siblings. Our childhood journeys were complex and difficult, and all of us had paid a price for our mother's struggles. When I met my sister Joni, I could see that struggle so clearly. Her demeanor was erratic and belligerent. She also evidently suffered from the struggles with alcohol that our mother had. Still, I wanted to embrace her; she was the only sister I had. But it became impossible when I realized that my sister was also an unapologetic racist. Our mother was white, and my father was African American; I had grown up as an African American man, something Joni could not understand or respect. Proud of my culture and with no tolerance for anyone who espoused racist views, I couldn't grasp that kind of hatred. Our relationship ended before it began when she called me a week after our first meeting to let me know that because I was African American, she would no longer speak with me. It remains our last conversation.

"There is something you should think about in regard to your sister," Carmen began when we finally connected. "When you were writing about her, you described the many difficulties she had as a child, including that she had been molested."

This was indeed true. One of the consequences of my mother's difficulties had been the loss of my sister's innocence. There was a long pause.

"Well," Carmen added quietly. "That happened to me too."

From the ages of seven to twelve, Carmen had been repeatedly molested by a family friend who went to great lengths to make sure she kept it a secret. Only when she was in middle school and asked a health education teacher questions that were beyond her years was anyone aware of what she had been enduring. When Carmen's mom learned what had been happening to her daughter, the man was prosecuted and sent to prison.

Her mom, devastated and wrestling with guilt, surrounded her with love, counseling, and support. But for Carmen the effect lingered on for many years.

"Something like that takes everything from you—your innocence, your joy, your entire sense of being. And when you are as young as I was, you don't have the language to describe what you are feeling. Throughout my high school and college years, I really struggled with a lack of self-worth. In my mind I became the 'not good enough' girl."

I listened quietly, stunned and amazed at Carmen's courage. I'd known her for several years by then and had always respected her as a working mother, balancing her career successes with her dedication to her husband and children as well as her mother and mother-in-law. And she did all that with a magnetic personality that was so authentic and genuine, she naturally drew people to her. Knowing now that she had overcome being sexually molested as a young girl and an avalanche of doubt that had nearly consumed her, only heightened my admiration for her. I was humbled that she would share that painful journey with me, and I told her so.

"I don't talk about it that much, but not because I'm ashamed. I'm so grateful that I'm okay now. My mom never left my side, and I married the man of my dreams, who helped me see my value. But clearly your sister was not as fortunate as I was. It doesn't make her views on race right—we both know she is quite wrong—but she's been terribly damaged, and it doesn't sound like anybody ever succeeded in trying to make her whole again."

As the writing process for this book unfolded, I continually checked with Carmen about publicly sharing this childhood experience. She could keep this painful memory to herself, after all. Each time I mentioned this, she would simply say, "Somebody out there might need to know there is a way through such a terrible experience, that they still have worth and value, and that they can heal enough to begin again." In her willingness to help others write a new chapter in their story, Carmen Ortiz-McGhee embodies the spirit and the essence of the lighthouse.

CHAPTER 7

WELLES REMY CROWTHER

Lord, teach me to be generous,
to serve as you deserve,
to give and not to count the cost,
to fight and not heed the wounds,
to toil and not to seek for rest,
to labor and not ask for reward,
save that of knowing that I do your holy will.
—PRAYER FOR GENEROSITY

Boston College is set in the leafy suburb of Chestnut Hill, Massachusetts, right outside Boston. It is one of forty-five institutions of higher learning in Boston, making the city one of the college capitals of the world. Several of the university's buildings are crowned Gothic towers, and they stand watch over the campus, protective guardians and humble observers of its history and traditions. The university has continually invested in the physical footprint of the campus, and the result is a picturesque mosaic of old stonework, manicured lawns, and shady trees. Boston College is commonly referred to as "The Heights," a reference to its elevated topography and symbolic of the university's motto: Ever to excel.

Much of the campus's beauty is channeled into the small stretch of road located at the university's entrance. When you first walk onto the main campus, Linden Lane welcomes you with a combination of idyllic nature and peaceful solitude. The lane is named for the lofty trees that line each side, their shade falling gently onto the path as students and faculty stroll past. At the end of the path, perfectly framed by the corridor of trees, stands the largest of the Gothic towers, Gasson Hall. As you get closer to this building, a column catches your eye, not so much the column as what sits atop of it: a shining golden eagle, its wings outstretched, a look of strength and determination emanating from its piercing eyes.

When you are a high school student trying to decide where you will spend the next four years of your life, something about the setting on Linden Lane whispers to you, quietly suggesting that this is the place. At least that's what it did for Welles Crowther. It was while he was passing by the campus with his mother, after visiting twenty-four other schools, that he first set his eyes on Linden Lane. In that moment, he decided he would attend Boston College. That moment turned out to be a near-perfect union of an exceptional young man, an extraordinary act of heroism, and a university that would honor that act, creating a light-house effect that will last for decades.

Welles Crowther's formative years were spent in Nyack, New York. He was one of three children of Alison and Jeff Crowther. The older brother to two younger sisters, Honor and Paige, Welles was an older brother not only by age but also by an innate sense of duty; he was always watchful and protective over his sisters. This wasn't something his parents ever needed to talk to him about; it came naturally to him. This sense of loyalty would become part of the fabric of his character and was reflected in everything he did, from his fondness for his extended family to the youth sports teams he was part of.

Perhaps that was why firefighting appealed so much to young Welles. From a young age, he was drawn to all aspects of the profession: the bright red truck with the long ladder, the loud siren announcing its arrival, the helmet sitting atop the head of the firefighter as if he or she were a conquistador. It was a love nurtured by his parents, through visits to the local firehouse, and furthered when Jeff, who worked in finance, began volunteering at Empire Hook & Ladder, one of the firehouses in Nyack. Not surprisingly, Welles tagged along and soon became part of the fraternity of firefighters.

This passion for the profession was not a childhood fancy, however. Rather, while many teenagers begin to step away from childhood loyalties, Welles stepped toward his. When he was sixteen, he joined Empire Hook & Ladder as a junior member. Two years later, he became a full member of the company, completing all the requisite training.

The college admissions process is a rite of passage for many high school seniors, a common life event that is vastly underestimated for its intensity and impact. Trying to find the best fit, worrying about gaining admission, and doing well enough on standardized tests dominate everyday conversations in school and at home. That the process plays out publicly does not help to ease the strain. It is a time of enormous transition, of moving on from one's high school years to the next stage of life. Yet there is also a poetic beauty to this process that can balance out the uncertainty. The college search opens you up to a bigger world, one filled with freedom and opportunities. You can imagine yourself in these new places, backpack slung over your shoulder, meeting new people and forming lifelong friendships.

At the time Welles Crowther was visiting Boston College, I was working on the admissions staff at the university. I took a great deal of pride in the work of being an admissions counselor, knowing that my signature on an acceptance letter could change the life of a young person. The world of college admissions can be an inexact science, but if you get it right, the talented applicant you accept will ultimately choose to attend your university. Though I wasn't directly responsible for accepting Welles to Boston College, I know he was exactly the kind of student we hoped would choose The Heights.

That he might enroll at Boston College was not a foregone conclusion. An honor student, two-sport athlete, and volunteer firefighter, Welles had a lot of wonderful options. He and his mother had already traveled all over the Northeast searching for the right fit and, more specifically, the moment the campus spoke to him and said, "You belong here." As they drove toward Boston College, Alison assumed that this visit would be like all the others. After all, the Crowthers were Episcopalian, and Boston College is a Jesuit Catholic institution, making a match even more unlikely. But then Welles saw Linden Lane and knew that this was the place he was supposed to be.

Whatever Welles was hoping his new home was, it turned out to be. He majored in economics, played lacrosse all four years, and developed strong friendships on the field and across the campus. He took advantage of the city's college culture, frequently jumping on the B line, the train that begins and ends at the southern end of the campus. Boston College prides itself on service, best reflected in the Jesuit calling to be "men and women for others."[1] Welles had come to Boston College with a spirit of helping, and the Fellowship of Christian Athletes, which he joined as a member of the lacrosse team, offered him an opportunity to continue to give back.

When Welles secured an internship with the investment banking firm of Sandler O'Neill & Partners in his sophomore year, it was part of a longer-term plan to work in the financial sector in New York City. After gaining more experience studying foreign markets in Spain during the summer of his junior year, he accepted an offer to join Sandler O'Neill full-time upon graduation.

His office was on the 104th floor of the South Tower of the World Trade Center.

Two years into his time at Sandler O'Neill, Welles appeared to be on the trajectory that might be expected of a twenty-four-year-old equities trader who was a quick study and willing to put in the extra work. Yet something nagged at him, something he couldn't fully articulate. Tom Rinaldi, in his beautifully written book, *The Red Bandanna*, reveals that Welles, though making great career progress in the financial sector, was still wrestling with his lifelong avocation of firefighting. In fact, after talking to his dad, he had gone so far as to request—and partially complete—an application to become a New York City firefighter. Maybe that's what our twenties are for—to make the decision between what the world tells us we *need* to do and what our heart *wants* to do. In a perfect world, there would be no decision to make because those two dimensions of our lives would be one and the same. But for Welles, those universes had not yet converged. Equity trading and firefighting are two vastly different worlds. In the former, one is immersed in analysis, research, and understanding how markets move and change. In the latter, one is trained to respond to distress, whether it be a car accident or a burning building. If there is any commonality to be found, it is in the sound that signals it is time to go to work; in the world of markets, it is the opening bell, and at the firehouse, it is the sound of the siren.

The morning of September 11 dawned bright and clear. All across the country, Americans were going about their daily routines, summer vacations replaced by school drop-offs and early-morning office arrivals. But that all changed when, at 8:46 a.m., the first of four hijacked airliners slammed into the North Tower of the World Trade Center. Seventeen minutes later, another airliner crashed into the South Tower, sixteen floors below Welles's office.

Alison and Jeff were going through their own daily routines; Jeff was at home getting ready for a charity golf tournament, and Alison was on her way to a business meeting about a half hour away. When the plane hit the South Tower, Welles called his dad, expecting him to be at his office. He left a message with his secretary instead. He then called his mother. Unable to reach her, he left the following message: "Mom . . . this is Welles. I . . . I want you to know that I'm okay." Nine minutes had elapsed since the plane had struck the South Tower.

Welles's message and his firefighter training gave his family and friends a brief glimmer of hope, knowing that Welles, of all people, would know what to do in such a dire emergency. But then the unimaginable happened: the South Tower, its structure severely compromised by the plane's impact and further weakened by the raging inferno, collapsed in a matter of seconds. Seeing the devastation of the collapse, the Crowthers, their extended families, and Welles's friends, all of whom had been contacting one another since the attack started, feared the worst.

Hours passed without any further word from Welles. The family stayed glued to the television. Unwilling to wait for news to come to him, Jeff went the following morning to the city, partly hoping to hear any word of what had happened to their son. At the same time, Alison was calling emergency rooms around the city, trying to see if any of the injured might possibly be Welles. Neither of these efforts, or the efforts of so many others in the Nyack community, were successful. Hours became days and with them came the harsh realization that Welles would not return home.

There was nothing left to do. On September 29, 2001, Welles's family and friends gathered at Grace Episcopal Church to remember and to grieve.

In the long course of coming to terms with a tragedy, we ultimately arrive at a stage of acceptance, however reluctantly. But for the Crowthers, acceptance would not fully come until Welles had been found. When recovery crews located Welles's body in March 2002, the Crowthers found some degree of comfort in knowing that Welles would be returned to Nyack. But the discovery brought other questions about what had unfolded that morning. They already knew quite a few details to create a timeline: he worked on the 104th floor; the plane struck the South Tower at 9:03 a.m., its impact spanning from the 78th to the 84th floor; he called his mother at 9:12 a.m. from his office to tell her he was okay; the tower collapsed at 9:59 a.m. But when his body was found with a group of firefighters who were last known to be in the lobby of the South Tower, they realized two things: first, he had made it down, and second, he was trying to help his fellow firefighters. What Alison and Jeff did not know, and it seemed would likely never know, is what occurred in those forty-seven minutes between Welles's message to his mom and the collapse of the South Tower.

That changed on Memorial Day weekend in 2002. We process grief in different ways; for Jeff, he wanted to stay as far away as possible from stories of that terrible day. It was enough that he felt the loss of his son each and every day. But 9/11 was a generational marker, one of those collective milestones so powerful that everyone remembers where they were when it happened. Avoiding it is incredibly difficult because the stories are everywhere you turn. So when the *New York Times* arrived at their home that Sunday morning, with its front-page story on the extraordinary battle for survival that unfolded in the towers, Jeff didn't want to read it. But for Alison, something was still unresolved, even though she couldn't put her finger on it. Reading every news account mattered, in part because she hoped to learn what her son had faced in those forty-seven minutes. She, and Jeff, would learn a lot more.

The *New York Times* story "Fighting to Live While the Towers Died" is a vivid recollection of that fateful morning's events.[2] Stringing together timelines, emails, phone messages, and survivor accounts, the article provides a stirring minute-by-minute account of what unfolded for those trapped in the towers after the airplanes struck. Reading it puts a human face to the desperation—and the bravery—of humanity in the most terrifying of moments.

As Alison was reading the article, a passage stopped her.

A mysterious man appeared at one point, his mouth and nose covered with a red handkerchief. He was looking for a fire extinguisher. As [survivor] Judy Wein recalls, he pointed to the stairs and made an announcement that saved lives: Anyone who can walk, get up and walk now. Anyone who can perhaps help others, find someone who needs help and then head down.

She froze. *This is Welles*, Alison knew. The words sounded like him and how he would have reacted in a crisis given his training as a firefighter. But the red handkerchief was the telltale sign. Years before, while getting ready for church, Jeff had presented Welles with two pieces of cloth, one white and the other red. "This one is for show," Jeff said, pointing to the white handkerchief, "and this one is for blow." He held up the red one. Welles eagerly accepted both gifts, but it was the red bandanna he was drawn to. It would become part of his identity, something beyond a good luck charm, always staying with him as he moved from childhood to adolescence to manhood. The word *bandanna* is believed to have originated from the Sanskrit word *badhnati*, which means "binds" or "ties." And for Welles that is what it would do: bind him to his father and, in a moment of extraordinary crisis, ultimately to his life's purpose.

The Crowthers likely would have never known of Welles's exploits were it not for the mention of the bandanna. But that is not all the *New York Times* reported. They also shared the names of survivors Judy Wein and Ling Young, who described in vivid detail their separate encounters with the young man they credited with saving their lives. Upon hearing the loud boom of the North Tower being struck, both women decided to evacuate their respective offices in the South Tower. They were standing in the lobby of the 78th floor, along with about two hundred others waiting for an elevator to take them down, when the second plane slammed into the South Tower, its wings angled as it disappeared into the building at 590 miles an hour.[3] The area where Ling and Judy were standing suddenly evaporated in a cloud of fire, smoke, and debris. The force of the impact threw them across the lobby, shattering Judy's arm and covering Ling's glasses with blood. Stunned and disoriented, Ling staggered to her feet. She could see that everything around her had flattened, including the walls of the once-beautiful lobby with its striking views of the New York City skyline. The blast had also leveled everyone who had been standing in the lobby only seconds before. As Ling looked around, she could see that the majority of those people had died instantly. Almost certainly in a state of shock, Ling did not move, unable to determine what to do next. That was when she heard a commanding voice directing her, and others who could stand, to the stairwell.

As the group proceeded down the stairs, Ling got a good look at the young man whose voice she had followed through the smoke, noting his T-shirt—and a red bandanna. She could also see that he had hoisted a woman over his shoulders in a fireman's carry. When they got below the damage of the impact, he set the woman down and told the group to keep going down to street level. But he would not join them. Remarkably, he went back up the seventeen flights of stairs to the lobby to see who else he could help. This time he encountered Judy Wein and another group of survivors and, as he had done on the first trip, summoned them to the stairwell and to safety.

In a crisis, the mind often takes snapshots, freezing the images of what we see and experience, going back to them again and again. This is certainly true when someone saves your life. When Alison reached out to Judy and Ling to show them a picture of Welles, they both confirmed what her mother's instinct already knew: the man in the red bandanna was indeed Welles. Out of the two hundred people waiting for an elevator on the 78th floor, only eighteen survived from at or above the impact zone in the South Tower, twelve of them because of Welles's bravery. They owe their lives to the man with the commanding voice, wearing a red bandanna, who emerged out of the smoke and darkness to guide them to safety.

The Lighthouse Effect: Selflessness

The lighthouse is perhaps the most selfless structure humankind has ever created. It does not exist to serve itself, nor can you pay it for the assistance it provides. It does not require acknowledgment, celebration, or commendation. It finds its reward in having guided the traveler toward safety and, in doing so, bending the arc of that life. This is not naive idealism on the part of the lighthouse; the harsh and dangerous elements where it exists are a daily reminder of the risks. And yet it is selfless anyway.

Purposeful Goodness

September 11, 2001, was a day marked by randomness. A missed flight, a canceled meeting, a late arrival to work, or what floor you worked on determined whether one lived or died.

From the moment the plane hit the South Tower, everything Welles did was for a purposeful good. He immediately called his parents to alleviate their concerns about his safety.

Even his tone of voice in issuing commands was filled with purpose because he certainly knew that people were disoriented and unsure what to do. Once he secured their safety, he went back up the stairwell at least twice more, looking for more survivors.

Purposeful acts of goodness mean showing kindness, consideration, empathy, and understanding, especially for people you don't know. It can be a physical act, but it can also be found in the way we interact with one another. We can be less critical in our words and less judgmental in our thoughts. We can show gratitude and kindness when we engage with another or when we work past perceived differences. Welles Crowther tried to live by this creed, never more than on the morning of September 11.

Find the Greater Good

The idea of the greater good, that we share a common space and therefore a common future, has been with us for centuries. But historically, there have been times when we undervalued how important this is and subsequently lost our way. We need to be reminded that our ability to overcome some of our biggest challenges as a country, and as a world, is found when we bond together. As a global pandemic unfolded in 2020, examples of those devoted to the greater good were all around us. Nurses and doctors performed their jobs with extraordinary courage, placing themselves in great peril while doing so. The scientific community came together to create a vaccine in record time, pulling humanity back from the precipice of a virus that has changed our way of life.

For some, serving the greater good is a need as primal as that of self-preservation. For Welles, in a moment of considerable crisis, the greater good came from his faith, the lessons instilled in him by Alison and Jeff, and the code of his firefighter training. Those on the front lines of the pandemic had signed up to save lives, and they intended to fulfill that mission, no matter the risk. At the core of their being is a driving emotion: *I will not leave you in your time of need.*

Sacrificing for Another

We often hear the word *sacrifice* used to describe what is necessary to achieve success in our personal lives. There is truth to this sentiment. To achieve our goals, we have to decide what we are willing to give up to realize those objectives. Many of us make these sacrifices knowing that it will bring us accomplishment and individual recognition. But the question for our world today is not what we will sacrifice for our own success but what we will sacrifice so that others might succeed. Answering this question requires temporarily putting aside our individuality and to be consistent in our empathy.

Consider for a moment Welles's decision-making process that fateful morning. He sacrificed his own safety to save others. This was not naive altruism on his part. As a trained firefighter, he was almost certainly aware of the implications of the catastrophic damage that the South Tower had sustained; firefighters are trained to understand the possibility of structural collapse of any building they enter. He had found his way to safety and could have simply continued toward the streets below. But he did not; he walked into the badly damaged lobby *looking* for someone to help. And yet even when he had secured the safety of some survivors, as well as his own, he kept going back up the stairs to see if he could save more. Like many of the 9/11 heroes who ran toward the danger, Welles considered his own well-being secondary.

Very few of us are called on in our daily lives to make the selfless decisions Welles made or to sacrifice all that he did. In retrospect, we now know that those decisions were matters of life and death. But we can take lessons from the example. We might sacrifice our time to support a worthy cause or wear a mask to help halt the spread of a life-threatening virus. We might change our consumption habits or the way we travel to address an ongoing climate crisis.

If we have any discomfort with foregoing conveniences to find that greater good, we should remind ourselves that we are all beneficiaries of those who surrendered comfort for our betterment. Perhaps it was a parent who worked multiple jobs to provide for the family; more broadly it might be a soldier who left their home and community to defend the country. When we remember why our own human lighthouses were so important to us, their willingness to sacrifice for us is one of the reasons we hold them in such high regard. And so we have a responsibility to consider the ways we can offer to others what they gave to us.

We must tell these stories of the 9/11 heroes not because we linger in the pain of their loss or because we want to canonize them but because their examples leave us with lessons on how we might live our life along the way.

That is why Welles's story continues to be told in articles, books, and documentaries. Like the lighthouse, it guides and informs. His name is memorialized at Grace Episcopalian Church in Nyack, at Empire Hook & Ladder, and at the 9/11 memorial in New York City. He inspired a curriculum taught in elementary and secondary schools and is the inspiration for the Welles Remy Crowther Charitable Trust, which "recognizes and awards academic and athletic excellence in young men and women who serve their communities and assists young people to become exemplary adults through education, health, recreation and character development."[4]

It is at Boston College that the legacy of Welles Crowther shines brightest. Each fall, at two separate times, the campus becomes a sea of red bandannas. One of these traditions is known as the Red Bandanna Game, when the Boston College football team takes to the field at Alumni Stadium, their uniforms decorated in the paisley pattern of the red bandanna. You can also see that same familiar pattern everywhere you turn: in the stands, on the sidelines, and on the field. On that day, the tradition and the pageantry of college football takes on an added dimension that is less about wins and losses and more about the impact of selflessness.

On another date, with the crispness of fall in the air, the beautiful campus framed by the foliage of the season, a smaller crowd gathers on the university's upper campus.

They are there for the annual Red Bandanna 5K Run, dedicated to Welles's memory and to support the work of the Welles Remy Crowther Charitable Trust. The red bandanna, now as familiar to the Boston College community as its official colors of maroon and gold, is everywhere to be seen, as is No. 19, the number Welles wore as a member of the lacrosse team. The starting line for the run is right in the middle of Linden Lane, the very place that spurred Welles to make his college choice.

But that is not the only place on Linden Lane where you can find the memory of Welles Crowther.

A lesser-known story about the aftermath of 9/11 is the number of colleges and universities that have honored the alumni they lost that fateful morning. Memorials and plaques of remembrance are found on college campuses all across the Northeast, from Pace University and Columbia University in New York City to the University of Hartford in Connecticut and the University of Vermont. The design of these memorials is unique, but all have a common feature: the name of the alumnus and the year they graduated.

For a campus that has seen so much transformation, Boston College's Linden Lane looks nearly identical to the way it did several decades ago, save for one subtle change. A few steps off the path, tucked into a quiet corner on the lawn behind Burns Library, is the memorial labyrinth. It is the university's 9/11 dedication to its twenty-two alumni, their names eternally etched into the smooth, gray stone. There you will find the name of Welles R. Crowther and, on occasion, a neatly folded red bandanna right under his name. The labyrinth is a place of contemplation and solitude, of reflective remembrance, a time to be present in the moment, an opportunity to slow down from life's hustling pace and to ponder what truly matters. It helps you along in this effort by asking you to take one step at a time. You need not worry about getting lost in the maze, however. The labyrinth speaks the eternal language of the lighthouse and personifies the spirit of Welles's final words: *Follow me, I know the way.*

CHAPTER 8

MONICA KACHRU AND RAJEEV TIPNIS

Grief is like a long valley, a winding
valley where any bend may reveal
a totally new landscape.
—C. S. LEWIS

In the summer of 2019, I announced my candidacy for the United States Senate, representing my home state of Massachusetts. I believed that I could bring a different set of life experiences to public service, one that reflected the challenges many Americans face every day. Those lives should have representation in Washington too. I also strongly believe we must all answer the call of country, however one defines that. Still, there was much about the political process I did not like. Endless hours of fundraising calls, a polarizing political culture that seemed so far removed from solving the challenges of everyday Americans, and a political system bent on stopping candidates were all disappointing. Nor did I care for the manufactured theater and stagecraft of politics, the deference and hero-worship expected for politicians when far too many of them do not deserve the adulation.

What sustained me was the campaign trail and meeting people from many different walks of life and hearing their stories. Their stories were my story. Alternatingly moved and inspired, I would leave campaign stops further reminded of the everyday heroes among us. Late at night, after the day had wrapped up, I would call Tonya and tell her stories of the people I'd met.

Knowing how much those exchanges lifted me was likely part of the reason Tonya informed the campaign that she was changing my schedule for the following week. This was met with respectful protests by the campaign team, who felt they owned my schedule—and ordinarily they would have been right. But our marriage has never worked on issuing edicts to one another. It has worked on trusting each other's instincts. Tonya clearly had strong feelings about my upcoming week, and I wanted to better understand why.

"Hey, T," I said pleasantly, walking over to a quiet corner, past a bright-blue "Pemberton for US Senate" sign. "You've excited quite a few folks over here."

"I got that sense," she replied. I could feel her smile through the phone. "But you're really needed at this event."

"Okay," I said. "Can you give me some context?"

For the next few minutes, she told me about a Needham,

Massachusetts, nonprofit foundation. Less than two years old, its mission is to increase the college graduation rates for first-generation students through one-on-one mentoring, financial assistance, and internship opportunities. These were the exact kind of support systems I needed during my college years, and I knew full well how arc-bending they could be to a young life trying to emerge from the shadows. But there was something more pressing, and I soon learned exactly what it was.

Monica Kachru grew up in Delhi, India, as part of a loving middle-class family. Her parents were wonderfully involved in her life, and education was a foundation of the family. Her father, a banker by training, encouraged her from childhood to find a place in the world where industries were not corrupt and hard work was valued. Though he had never been, he believed that promised land existed in only one place: the United States. Over the years, dinner conversations frequently included a discussion about the magical foreign land over 7,300 miles away.

Meanwhile, in Gwalior, India, several hours away, a similar conversation was unfolding in the Tipnis household. The youngest of three siblings, Rajeev showed an early aptitude for the sciences. Some of this affinity came from his parents, his mother a lecturer of psychology and his father a professor of physics. Rajeev's father was among the first of the Fulbright Scholars from India to come to the United States in the 1960s.

Rajeev earned his engineering degree in electronics and communication while attending Delhi Institute of Technology and Management in New Delhi. But America still beckoned. Inspired by his father and encouraged by what he read in the Institute of Electrical and Electronics Engineers magazines regarding science, technology, and engineering advancements rapidly evolving in Silicon Valley, Rajeev applied to colleges in the US. He had a major problem, though: lack of money. Without a scholarship or an assistantship, Rajeev would not be able to attend an American university even if he was accepted. The solution came when his father gave him the money, enough for a single semester but barely enough on which to survive. He decided to attend Michigan Technological University, where he saw snow (and lots of it) for the first time. Armed with only enough funds for one semester, Rajeev continued his quest for an assistantship while working in the cafeteria and taking other odd jobs to make ends meet.

Finally, he caught a break when Worcester Polytechnic Institute in Massachusetts offered him an assistantship to teach and research. There he found a lot more than that, including a community of friends from his native land. He traveled back to India to see his parents whenever his budget allowed. He had also become interested in the younger sister of one of his friends and would often send presents to her. One time he stopped by to say hello, and in the course of that conversation, they discovered they had similar interests and aspirations and values.

That conversation was the start of Monica and Rajeev's relationship, and they began to spend more time with each other. As their relationship grew, communication was difficult, especially when she was in India and he was in the States. Their love story started before email, texting, and social media, which meant making costly international phone calls at around $1.20 per minute. Monica jokes that these calls became the catalyst for Rajeev's marriage proposal. The solution, after careful cost-benefit analysis, including the expensive phone bills, was to get married sooner rather than later. Monica was twenty-two and Rajeev was twenty-four. They were married in Delhi on August 9, 1993, surrounded by family and friends.

After their wedding they returned to the United States, moving often within Massachusetts. As immigrants, they were focused on getting settled, trying to find their place, their community. While Rajeev had some connections in academia, for Monica the transition was more difficult. She missed her friends desperately. She experienced culture shock and social shock, the kind that makes one quietly ask, "What am I doing here?" They often talked about moving back to India, but in the end, they both loved the work they were doing in the US. Massachusetts had plenty of employment opportunities for both of them, considerably more than India. That is the immigrant's reality—they go where the opportunities take them, knowing they might arrive in a place that fulfills their needs but not all their wants.

Rajeev and Monica began planning for children and discovered that even preparing for a baby was different. In their native India, there were no formal sessions on how to have a baby or what to expect during pregnancy. They simply learned from their mothers and aunts and other women in their families. Soon pamphlets for Lamaze classes and books about pregnancy lay about their home, further reminders of their new world. Before they knew it, they were parents to two girls: first Anaya in 1998 and then Aisha in 2001.

Being a mother only intensified what Monica wanted—community. Rajeev immersed himself in work and had found community among local technology entrepreneurs. For Monica it had remained elusive, exacerbated by the conflict she felt as a working mother who wanted to be home with her children. And then, when she least expected it, she found community in an unlikely place—on the basketball court. She had fallen in love with the game in India, so when a group of women who played pickup basketball invited her to play, she readily accepted. In many ways, this collection of suburban women reminded her of her friends back in India. They became a turning point for her, for she had finally found a familiar tribe in a foreign land.

Fully settled, Monica and Rajeev set about raising their daughters. Anaya and Aisha became the center of Monica and Rajeev's life, much as Monica and Rajeev had been for their parents. Working hard, being authentic, being honest and trustworthy, and making one's own way result in merit, in value—these were values they modeled, discussed in their home, and instilled in their children. In their home, discussions focused on hard work and values. At the dinner table, the family would debate religion, feminism, music, politics, and any other topic of the day.

The girls were quite different from each other. Aisha, typical of most children, would often ask for the newest doll or dress. Anaya was more of an old soul, unusually thoughtful and sensitive. She would always take the extra steps needed to offer care and empathy to others. When Rajeev's mother, her grandmother, passed away, Anaya offered support to her dad, but she was also quite curious about where people go when they die.

Anaya always wanted to be involved in some project or other. Each project she chose needed to have a grand impact at its conclusion. For Anaya, there were no simple projects; each project she took on had to be a "big thing." Everything she did had to be done at the highest level, had to have the greatest effect, to have an impact, to be felt, to be seen, to make a difference. Anaya often told her mom that she wished she were forty years old so she could hang out with Monica's friends as well as her own. It was all a part of who she was.

Anaya particularly enjoyed writing, which captured her essence. Her essays were incredibly well-written and thought-provoking for one so young. Her teachers often commented on her writing, saying they fully expected to see her books in bookstores of the future. Academically, she excelled. Personally, she was loved by teachers and fellow students.

She was also quite competitive, continually pushing herself out of her comfort zone. She saw every situation and circumstance as an opportunity to lean in. Monica often felt exhausted just being Anaya's mom, believing she simply couldn't keep up with her. Anaya wanted to create social media events to bring kids from other cultures together, and she wanted Monica to help. Monica confessed she couldn't; the projects were just too big.

When Anaya applied for colleges, she was accepted into many amazing schools—Dartmouth, Brown, MIT, and more. Few things capture Anaya's spirit more than her MIT essay in response to being asked to share what she did in her free time, as if there is ever such a thing for someone so driven.

> I beat box! I have always loved Rap Music. Rap is more than poetry; it is word play with cadence and meter amplified by the din of the beat. A rapper is a swaggering Shakespeare, their words are the soliloquy, the beats the stage, the arts' ambition. Fascinated, I taught myself to mimic the clicks of a snare, turn up the bass, unveil the saxophone. To my friends delight and my family's exasperation, I can spontaneously erupt into a human symphony. I have even started writing my own rhymes. It is incredibly fun to drop a beat and try something completely new.

The university she ultimately chose to attend, MIT, was soon going to have a swaggering Shakespeare of their own.

But it was not to be. On August 11, a few weeks before she was to start college, Anaya ended her life.

The sudden, unexpected loss of such a bright light was devastating to all who knew Anaya. As a family, they struggled with feelings of enormous guilt. What didn't they see? They recalled their last few conversations, turning them over, searching for some clue that could explain the tragedy. One month before, Anaya told her mom she wanted to be a monk and that her purpose was perhaps to shed her ego and love everyone unconditionally. At the time, Monica did not understand what she meant and was worried; Anaya was nineteen and Monica didn't know any nineteen-year-old who spoke like that. Later that day Monica asked Anaya if she still wanted to be a monk and whether she had looked into it seriously. Anaya made an offhand joke and dismissed her earlier comment. At the time, Monica was relieved she had been joking and dismissed it as well. But now Monica realized how profound a statement that had been, that at such a young age Anaya was searching for the meaning of life and may have been questioning whether she should go to college. Rajeev wondered if the selection of the university was a contributing factor. Though Anaya was excited by her acceptance, even making an immediate shopping trip to purchase MIT merchandise, did the anxiety of attending a prestigious university overwhelm her?

Each day they woke up racked by questions of "What if?" Were there any signs? Had they pushed her to this place? What if they had raised her in India or another part of the United States? What if they had sent her to a different school? What if they had slowed down her relentless pursuit of excellence by emphasizing the beauty of each day?

Monica explains the initial overwhelming grief and the devastating feelings of guilt:

> Losing a child kills a part of you forever. It leaves a hole so wide that it swallows you. In an instant all the years of your life—holding and carrying Anaya, watching her grow, juggling PTA meetings and work, helping her with homework, cooking her dinner—they are suddenly gone, snatched away as if they were never lived. We

wondered what we did wrong. Maybe we didn't deserve her. Maybe we didn't respect her soul the way we should have. Maybe we didn't say to her enough that we loved her and we'd never be the same if anything happened to her. If she would have known how much this would crush us and her sister, she would never have done it. It was our job to protect her and we failed her.

Monica and Rajeev's experiences in America are reflections of the nation itself. For most who come to America as an immigrant, there is a covenant, an understanding of what is required to succeed: hard work is crucial, as a matter of survival and as a value. These were the values that had been instilled in Monica and Rajeev, the right ones they were supposed to have, *needed* to have, and that had to be passed on to their children. Anaya embodied this sentiment, perhaps may have had it in overdrive. Had those same values cost them their beloved Anaya?

The hard truth is that no answers were forthcoming if they were to be found at all, for no reply was going to bring Anaya back to them. Fear, anxiety, grief, anger, and guilt hit them in waves. They found themselves adrift in a never-ending storm of pain, the kind of pain that bends a soul and leaves one questioning every truth they've ever held.

For Aisha, the loss of her older sister was incredibly hard. As a child, Aisha would wait every day to walk with Anaya to school and play with her afterward. As the older sister, Anaya was very loving toward and protective of Aisha, another strong maternal influence in her life. Days before ending her life, she had promised Aisha that she would never hurt herself. Now that she was gone, Aisha felt a similar anguish as her parents and a deep sense of isolation. Not wanting to interrupt the high school normalcy of her friends' lives, and wanting to brighten the lives of her family, Aisha never talked about the tragedy at all.

This silence coupled with the overwhelming sadness, and the only way Aisha found it possible to continue day to day was by being in denial. This was a dangerous strategy. She and her therapist would talk about it and how with time she would have to allow the sadness to come and how she would one day have to process her grief. Aisha's junior and senior years were a blur. But as she came to the end of her high school years, graduating from high school and getting accepted into college, she found herself at a point in life in which she deeply felt Anaya's absence. It was the time of life in which Anaya had struggled most, and now Aisha found herself at eighteen years of age, struggling. She finally had to acknowledge the extent of her pain. She spoke honestly and vulnerably with her therapist, processing her grief and finding more clarity in her life.

Help came from an unexpected place. The Needham community poured their support into Monica and Rajeev's family, unwilling to let them bear the pain alone. One acquaintance, who they knew only in passing, occasionally showed up at their home with fruit baskets often would take walks with Monica. The grieving couple frequently had dinner at another neighbor's home, their conversations extending well into the evening. Each Saturday, a group of four friends invited themselves over to Monica and Rajeev's home, armed with recipes and food. Without asking Monica and Rajeev's permission, they rooted around in the kitchen for pots and pans, and soon enough, a cooking class was born. Later on, Monica and Rajeev would learn that these efforts had been carefully planned and coordinated. For Monica and Rajeev, it would come to redefine what community and friendship really mean.

Monica and Rajeev had no idea they were so loved. They experienced the kind of support they had longed for when they first came to the United States, and that love carried them in a time when all seemed lost. For Monica, this outpouring reinforced her belief in the goodness of humanity and affirmed a truth she long held to be true: compassion can move us past our differences.

As a family, they had not fully understood the impact Anaya had in the community. Shortly after Anaya's passing, a neighbor, Gretchen, showed up at their home with a card. She introduced herself to Monica and Rajeev, saying, "You don't know me, but Anaya used to teach my children math." Though they knew Anaya had been tutoring young people, they were unaware who those students were. Gretchen continued to drop by, simply to check in on them. They told her they were moved by her efforts but that she didn't need to do so much. Gretchen responded, "No, no—this is personal." She explained to them that Anaya had been teaching her children for free because she wanted them to love math. Now her children were going to school majoring in math, a choice she attributed to Anaya's influence.

The warmth of the community's embrace awakened Monica and Rajeev to a way through their grief. The whisper of how they could best remember Anaya became a roar when they reread her final note. She thanked her parents for giving her everything she needed and wanted. She told them that she would always be with them. The majority of her letter was about what they should do next. Anaya's last wishes were that her parents help young people and specifically to "help make their dreams come true." So was born the Anaya Tipnis Foundation.

From the outset, Monica and Rajeev felt that the foundation, in its intention and its impact, needed to match the grief and loss they felt and Anaya's intensity of spirit. They harkened back to Anaya's love of learning and their own fundamental belief in the power of education. Nine out of ten first-generation college students do not walk across the graduation stage because of a combination of financial, social, and support challenges. This, they believed, was the work that Anaya would want them to do.

Gretchen, Monica and Rajeev's persistent neighbor, wasn't done being persistent. While having dinner at a mutual friend's home, she noticed an invitation to a campaign event I was hosting. Gretchen reached out to a mutual friend who contacted Tonya to tell her about the foundation and the event I would be asked to speak at.

When I stepped into Temple Beth Shalom in Needham that warm August night, I could see the very community that had embraced Monica, Rajeev, and Aisha in their time of need. College students, community advocates, faith leaders, and members of the business community had all gathered to bestow the foundation's first scholarships on soon-to-be college students at Clark University, UMass Amherst, and Dartmouth College. I smiled quietly when I noticed that

Monica's dress and Rajeev's shirt were the exact same shade of blue. Rajeev and I exchanged a long handshake and a wordless knowing look that comes from fathers who adore their daughters. Monica addressed the small gathering and offered powerful remarks on the importance of supporting this vulnerable population suddenly thrust into the new world of college. I followed, sharing my perspective as a once-vulnerable college student, the intervening years having taught me how important the Anaya Tipnis Foundation was going to be for these scholars and the many more they will serve in the years to come.

On the foundation's website is this moving tribute to Anaya's legacy:

Each one of us has the power to leave a positive imprint on others. Anaya left a permanent imprint on the hearts and minds of everyone she touched and inspired us to build a village of support around young scholars in need. Through a tuition scholarship, school admissions mentoring, academic tutoring, and other assistance, The Anaya Tipnis Foundation fully embraces its scholars.

Unique, humble, and selfless with a quiet regal poise, Anaya was a young woman who understood the privileges education and supportive family and community provided, and felt all young people deserved an opportunity to prosper through higher education and a strong support system.

As the meaning of her name conveys, God answered, Anaya's life was marked by a nobleness of generosity, warmth, and joy. The Anaya Foundation's mission and ethos are hers. We are driven by who she was and the change she hoped for the world. Welcome to Anaya's village.[1]

The Lighthouse Effect: Strength and Honor

Fewer subjects are harder to talk about than suicide, in part because of the lack of understanding of the subject and the overwhelming feeling of guilt that suicide survivors often feel. As a society, we are slowly changing our attitudes and perceptions of suicide, in part because of people like Monica and Rajeev, who courageously share their stories.

Mental health remains an ongoing crisis, accelerated by a global pandemic. It is estimated that over one million people across the world die from suicide each year.[2] That number, according to research, is twice the number of lives lost to homicide. It is also one of the leading causes of death among young people. I still have not fully found the words to convey my admiration and respect for Monica and Rajeev and their willingness to share their journey. Though it is difficult, I know part of the reason they are doing so is that they hope others will see a way to move forward in their own lives.

Offer Your Presence

When someone we care about is hurting, our first instinct is to reach out and be supportive. In the immediate aftermath of a struggle or loss, there is a wonderful rush of support. As time moves on, we go back to our normal lives, but our grieving friend can't because their life is no longer normal. A void exists where something important once was, and it will take a long time before they can find anything approaching normalcy again. That is why having a continued presence in their lives is so important. We could clearly see this in Monica and Rajeev's story, especially when the Needham community continually reached out to connect with the two of them. And they have never stopped; that same community continues to lift the family by supporting Anaya's village. Volunteers mentor the scholars, host internships to introduce them to the world of work, and assist these future leaders with the college admissions process.

Much is written about finding strength in times of great difficulty. Far less is written about how we can be a source of strength for someone in their time of need. For some of us, we might not know what to say in a moment of grief and are afraid of saying the wrong thing. But we don't have to have all the words, because the truth is that sometimes there aren't any. And that's okay. Sometimes our presence alone is strength enough. A hand to hold or a wordless walk can be more helpful than anything we say.

Honor Life

There is no recovery from the loss of a child to a mental health crisis. It leaves a void that can be neither filled nor replaced. But Monica and Rajeev consciously decided they would honor their daughter's life and remember her spirit by improving the lives of others. The scholarship award winners I met and the many that will follow are the grateful beneficiaries of Anaya's final wishes. They will graduate from college with the support of Anaya's village and, I suspect, will find joy in their personal and professional lives. As they do, they will positively impact lives as their own have been impacted. Though Anaya is not here to fulfill her own dreams, those who take up the baton for her are helping others to achieve theirs, thereby continuing her legacy.

Those who tended and cared for the lighthouse had no greater responsibility than to preserve the powerful light that shone so brightly out into the sea. Monica and Rajeev show us how to keep a light burning. They remind us that when we honor a life, we remember what they meant to us and keep a part of their light with us always. They also show us that we can share a loved one's light and even have a responsibility to do so. We can do this by speaking their name and telling their stories, or we can take up the work they would have wanted to do had they been granted more time. We can remember them at their brightest: the way they smiled or laughed or the times they made us do the same. We can remember they loved us despite our imperfections and that we loved them despite theirs. Even in our grief, we can honor their lives by continuing to live our own to the fullest extent possible and helping others do the same. They would want that for us. All these memories remind us that they were here with us once and that the trajectories of our lives have unfolded in part because they were with us at all. We loved them then and we love them still.

CHAPTER 9

CLAIRE LEVIN

*A society grows great when its
elders plant trees
In whose shade they know
they shall never sit.*
—GREEK PROVERB

In the Pemberton home, Sunday dinner is a time to catch up after a long week of homework, meetings, and practices. As the kids have gotten older and their schedules have gotten busier, it's been the only time we're able to sit together as a family. The five of us gather at our small kitchen table, and each of us talks about their past week and the week up ahead. Milo, our miniature goldendoodle, frolics about our feet, hoping that one of the kids will sneak him some table food.

Given my busy travel schedule, the kids always enjoy

hearing where I will be going that particular week. That is why they save me for last. But one particular time I was hoping they would forget me altogether, something I tried to help along by trying to change the conversation.

But Quinn, our oldest son, whose cheerful disposition often disguises a more reflective personality, wasn't having it. "Not so fast, Dad," he said. "Your turn."

"Well," I paused, "I'm going to Washington, DC, to speak at a conference."

"What kind of conference this time?" Vaughn, our younger son, asked. Mischievous and insightful, he sensed there was another story.

I hesitated even longer this time. "It's a women's conference actually." I winced as I said this because I knew what was coming next.

"Hold on," Kennedy, our daughter, said. "Here it comes," I thought. The youngest in birth order, she had come into the world and promptly staged a takeover. "*You're* speaking at a women's conference?"

Eyebrows shot up around the table. Tonya gave me a look that said, *You're in trouble now.* I looked at my sons with a "help me out here" expression. "You're on your own" shoulder shrugs greeted me in reply.

I was about to answer when Kennedy chimed in with another question.

"No offense, but couldn't they find a girl?"

We all burst out laughing. She had a point, one that I had been wrestling with myself. When the invitation came from my friend who was leading the conference, I had politely declined. The last person a room of women, all accomplished in their own right, needed to hear from was a man. But my friend had persisted, indicating that it was important for men to be heard on matters of gender equity.

Still, I wanted to offer something more meaningful than a message of general support. For days I had pondered how to approach my remarks. What if I shared a story about a woman who touched my life? I called my friend and shared my idea, and she readily agreed. Of course, I'd already had an idea of whom I wanted to talk about. In many ways, she was the perfect choice.

Claire Elias was born and raised in Brooklyn, New York. Her mother and father had emigrated from Turkey and were part of a sect of the Jewish faith referred to as Sephardic Jews, who came to the US in large numbers in the early 1900s. Cast out of Spain in the fifteenth century, Sephardic Jews, as the story goes, are direct descendants of King David. They speak a unique dialect, a combination of Spanish and Yiddish, and follow unique customs. New York City, already a collection of European clans fleeing persecution and seeking greater opportunity in America, would be their primary place of settling. This is where Claire would grow up, in the Sheepshead Bay neighborhood of Brooklyn.

Her childhood was typical of that of a first-generation American, whose work ethic and own customs and traditions went hand in hand. She attended James Madison High School at the same time as future Supreme Court Justice Ruth Bader Ginsburg. But when Claire was sixteen years old, her father, Solomon, fell ill and the family began to struggle financially. Faced with few options, the family moved to New Bedford, Massachusetts, where Claire's uncle was a successful businessman. He owned an entire mill complex that ran alongside New Bedford's waterfront as the historic city continued its transition from whaling to weaving.

Claire moved to New Bedford ahead of her family so that she could start school at the beginning of the year. The plan was for Claire's parents to follow later. In addition to starting school in a new city far away from her friends, Claire would also be working for her uncle in the bustling garment industry.

On her first day of high school, Claire walked to the bus stop equal parts anxious and excited. Perhaps that was why she had dropped her book bag. As she kneeled to pick up the bag's contents, a boy walked up to the bus stop. He asked if she needed help, but she politely declined. The boy had never seen her before, so Claire explained she had just moved to the area and was staying with her uncle. He knew of the family, as they did not live too far from him. Claire also shared that her family would be arriving later.

For Fred, it was love at first sight, but he was younger than Claire by two years and a freshman no less. In the all-important world of high school, such a relationship would be frowned upon, especially for the new girl in town. Still, they saw each other often in the neighborhood and remained friendly. Upon graduation Claire went to work in her uncle's office, helping him keep the books. Fred joined his father as a rag picker, the trade of those who collected unused rags from clothing factories, sorting them and selling them wherever they could find a market. Soon they expanded their practice to scrap metal and then fishing nets. In the oceanside community of New Bedford, with deep ties to the sea, there would always be a market for fishing nets. Meanwhile, Claire and Fred's friendship blossomed into a love story; they married in 1959, and then their three sons, Howie, Steve, and Jerry, were born within a span of five years.

Fred turned his attention full-time to the fishing net business. Claire joined him as his bookkeeper. As their family grew, the young family moved to the west end of New Bedford. Their modest home offered a short walk to the elementary school, the local park, and downtown New Bedford. Their young boys were the center of their lives, and the children kept their parents busy with their many childhood pursuits, from baseball games to summer camps. Often Fred and Claire would walk to Sunnybrook Farms, the local neighborhood convenience store, to buy a few household items or the evening newspaper. Sometimes while Fred was at work and the boys were at one activity or another, Claire would take the walk herself, enjoying the quiet of the day.

That was where I first encountered her, as I was seated on a rock wall across the street from my latest foster home.

I'd been in an orphanage and several other foster homes before I arrived in the neighborhood in 1972, just a few weeks after my father's murder, though I don't know if those two events were directly related. My mother, though alive, was in the middle of a losing battle with alcoholism and almost certainly fighting a mental health crisis as well. She had lost legal custody of me, and my siblings and I were never to see her again.

The three-tenement building that I now called home

looked terribly out of place on the tree-lined street. Taller than any other home by far, it was a monstrosity, some kind of architectural mistake that seemed to mock the rest of the neighborhood. I tried to stay out of the home as much as possible, escaping to the outdoors, often with one of my few books in hand. When Claire Levin approached me one summer afternoon, she did not know the true nature of the home or what unfolded behind closed doors. What she did know was that I liked to read. The rock wall was my favorite place to do so, as it was away from the foster home that often functioned more like a prison.

"What are you reading there?" she asked.

I hesitated. Talking to adults was risky. The foster family lived in a world of deceit and manipulation, especially when it came to me. "You are never to tell anyone what goes on here. Unwanted kids like you disappear all the time and nobody asks any questions." Any adult I encountered would send me into a spat of anxiety. *What if they start asking me questions?*

I gulped hard. In my nervousness, I did not respond to her question and simply held up my latest Encyclopedia Brown mystery. Leroy Brown, known to his friends as Encyclopedia for his vast knowledge, was a boy detective who often helped his father, the chief of police in the fictional seaside town of Idaville. He solved mysteries that had stumped the police department. I loved any kind of mystery, from Sherlock Holmes to Nancy Drew, but I especially liked Encyclopedia, in part because he was a boy my age. And like him, I was trying to solve a mystery too—except mine was the mystery of where I had come from.

"You like mysteries?" she asked.

"Oh yes, ma'am," I responded. "I really like how you get a chance to figure out the clues for yourself."

"Now, if I remember, weren't you reading this book last week?"

On more than one occasion, I had noticed her as she walked through the neighborhood. It hadn't occurred to me that she had noticed me too. Another wave of anxiety hit me. I wondered what else might she have seen. Would the foster family think I was talking to her and telling her what was really happening to me in that home?

I had to come up with an answer that wouldn't give me away.

"Yes, ma'am. But when I finish a book, I go back to the beginning and start all over again."

"I see." She said nothing more and continued her walk toward the store. I watched her walk away, trying to solve the mystery of how she knew I was reading the same book over and over again.

That evening, while in the middle of my evening chores, I heard a knock at the door. The foster mother answered, and a voice I recognized immediately asked, "Is Steve here? I have something I would like to give him." What she had to give me was a box of books, which she brought me not only that night but many times until I left that neighborhood at sixteen, on my way to live with John Sykes. When I left that cold December morning with my social worker, Mike Silvia, the only meaningful possessions I had were several of the books she had given me.

Reading is a real-life superpower. It transports and transforms. The books Claire Levin offered became a magical escape, taking me to enchanted places that the foster family could never go. They never denied the books coming into the home because to do so would have raised suspicions. These texts were not just words but rather entire worlds I could get lost in where there was joy and laughter and love. They gave me vision and a way to get beyond the place I lived—a cold, hard dwelling devoid of kindness and caring. Once I saw this other world, its promise and its possibilities, I couldn't unsee it, for this human lighthouse had unknowingly lit a path through the darkness.

We never forget who sees us first. For many of us, that person is Mom or Dad, Grandma or Grandpa. But for some of us, inheritors of a tragedy not of our making, that look comes from a kind stranger who stops to truly see us, not the circumstances of our life but its possibilities.

In my first book I tried to capture how important Claire Levin had been to me because I could never forget her. As time and life moved on, and the joyful world I often read about in the books she offered actually came to pass for me, my gratitude for what she did only intensified. When I left that neighborhood, I made a quiet promise that I would never return to the place where so much pain and suffering had unfolded. Years later I broke that promise, and it was for only one reason: I wanted to find Claire Levin. But I was too late; when I rang the bell of the home on Maple Street, I learned that she and her family had left that neighborhood several years earlier. The home's new residents had no idea where she had moved.

In the course of writing *A Chance in the World*, I had solved quite a few mysteries, from what had happened to my mother and father to the origins of my strange birth name, Steve Klakowicz. But I had not been able to find Claire Levin. Many years had passed, and I begrudgingly accepted that it simply was not meant to be. Nevertheless, I could still tell the story of what her kindness had meant and how it had bent the arc of my life. I could show how that story had inspired many others to have a similar impact, from a book drive in Indianapolis that resulted in donations of more than one million books to literacy efforts in schools all across the country. Since I couldn't find her and thank her in person, telling her story at events like these would have to do.

I arrived at the women's leadership conference, which was being held in the majestic Gaylord National Resort in National Harbor. It was late October and autumn was in full swing. There was a crispness in the air, and the many hues of fall had descended on the nation's capital, providing a colorful backdrop to the regal, pristine white buildings. I had been looking forward to the conference despite the kids' continued good-natured teasing about my speaking at a conference for women. But I knew I would be welcomed there among colleagues and friends I respected and admired. I also had a plan that would make this conference address particularly special.

Telling the story of Claire Levin never gets tiring because the memory of her never gets old. I approached the podium and, after a few comments of appreciation, told the story of the power of a box of books. A hush had fallen over the large room, and it grew even quieter as I read one of my favorite passages from *A Chance in the World*:

> In my quiet moments of reflection, I often wonder what might have become of me had not this kind woman lit a pathway for me through the suffocating darkness of the house on Arnold Street. . . .
>
> I do not know where Mrs. Levin is today, and neither she nor her family knows what has become of me. I don't even know if Levin was her real name, but that was the name penned inside the covers of many of the books she gave me. For the rest of my childhood, however, she would walk beside me. And as an adult I have found that I cannot forget her.[1]

To write down words is one thing, to speak them to a room full of people is another matter entirely. The voice now does the job that the pen would ordinarily do. But giving voice to a personal experience can overwhelm you; you relive the moment and the significance of it all over again. As I finished the passage, I struggled to maintain my composure.

There was another reason for this, something virtually no one else knew: Claire Levin was in the room listening to my remarks.

Shortly after my first book's publication, I received a series of phone calls from a childhood friend who lived in the neighborhood. He'd read my descriptions of Mrs. Levin and set about trying to find her and her family. It took a few phone calls and the help of a local rabbi, but soon enough, he located the woman who, up until then, had been unaware of the story that was circulating about her.

Talking with Claire Levin some thirty years after I last saw her remains one of my great joys. Shortly after that phone call, Tonya and I traveled to Dartmouth, Massachusetts, to sit down with her and her extended family, which included her sons, their wives, and several grandchildren.

Doing so offered me the opportunity to ask her something that had always been on my mind. I'd known what she had done, but I had not known *why*. This wasn't a singular act of kindness in which she'd been engaged but something she'd done for over a decade. I suspected that there were some life lessons in there for me—and for all of us.

What I came to learn about Claire Levin is that much of the way she showed up in the world was because of her mother's influence. Unable to read or write, Claire's mother could still knit a sweater without a pattern, keep a mental catalog of a long list of recipes, and speak several languages, including English and Greek as well as her native dialect. She was also a giving person, who even as she aged would cash her social security check and give a bit away to everyone in her family.

Claire possessed something else as well, something her own children began to see at an early age. Strangers would often strike up a conversation with her. Still others would confide in her, seeking her counsel when they experienced difficulty. Was it her warm smile, the one that always seemed to reach her eyes? Perhaps, but it was also her spirit; being in Claire's presence was like sitting by a cozy fire on a cold winter day, its warmth providing comfort against the chill.

She had a sixth sense for knowing who needed help and

when they needed it. She was often called on by the local elementary school principal, Mrs. Walsh, to come and sit with children at the school who needed support. No matter what the problem was, Claire would always come, as if a substitute school psychologist.

Whether it was books or her time, giving was not something Claire Levin did; giving was simply who she was. Private in nature and not needing to be celebrated, she was unaware of how much of an impact she'd had, and if she was aware, she likely would not have told anyone. This was the woman I tried to describe to the conference-goers:

> Women like Claire Levin are to be found in the history of all our families, humble women whose sacrifices were not always fully understood or appreciated in their time. They often toiled in factories and low-paying jobs while raising a family, many times sacrificing their own career aspirations to do so. They are our great-grandmother and grandmother, our mother and our aunt. They exist in our family stories as sources of pride, and our appreciation for them shows up in the way we live our lives today and the stories we tell our daughters about them. It is our way of saying thank you for all that they have done—and the path they have lit for us. We know that the only reason we exist is because of them.

I talked about Claire's life, the kind of wife and mother she was, the tireless dedication to her family, and the extraordinary compassion that marked her life, of which I was a particular recipient. I continued on:

There is not a day that passes that I don't say thank you to Claire Levin, especially on a day like today. So I'm going to say thank you again, but this time I am going to ask you to help me, because Claire Levin is here with us today.

When I initially received the invitation to speak at the conference, I reached out to the Levin family to see whether she would be interested in being my special guest. Though they were thrilled by the offer, the Levin family had to give it some thought. Claire rarely left their neighborhood and had not been on an airplane in fifty years. Struggling with an ailing hip, she was also now wheelchair-bound. We worked on a travel plan together to make sure she would be comfortable, and her daughter-in-law Susan and grandson Danny would travel with her for support.

The room paused, trying to discern whether they had heard me correctly. But then I gestured in Claire's direction, and a small light shone on where she sat. The women jumped to their feet in a cacophony of room-shattering applause, sending a wave of appreciation that washed over her. After a few moments I tried to speak, but the room only became louder, drowning out my voice. From the stage, I watched Claire smile and wave to the crowd, which ignited yet another rousing ovation.

For the next half hour, a steady stream of well-wishers greeted her. Many of them had tears in their eyes as they knelt beside her wheelchair. Though they did not know her personally, they knew women like her, those on whose sacrifices they now stood. In acknowledging her, they were also remembering the women who had paved an important path for them.

After the morning session of the conference wrapped up, Claire and her family spent the remainder of the day touring Washington, DC, seeing historical sites that, up to that point, she had seen only on television. Not too long after the conference, she began to show signs of dementia. As her health declined, Claire's family surrounded her with all the love they could muster for their family matriarch. After eighty-two trips around the sun, she passed away peacefully in 2016.

Claire Levin was a human lighthouse in my storm. Her light, her life, and the example of it carry on.

The Lighthouse Effect: Giving What You Can

"Hey you, hey you," the frail voice said, beckoning the young woman to her car.

It was mid-March 2020, and COVID-19 had begun its deadly trek throughout the US, sending citizens across the country scrambling for supplies for what proved to be a long, arduous fight. The people most vulnerable were the elderly, which is why the two people in the car dared not get out of their vehicle. "We need help," said the elderly woman. "We need to get groceries, but we're afraid to go inside. We've been here forty-five minutes waiting to ask the right person for help." She rolled down her window just a little more and gingerly held out her grocery list along with a hundred-dollar bill. "Would you mind going into the store to get these things for us?"

The young woman said, "Of course."

She went inside, purchased the supplies, and brought them back out to the couple, placing the groceries in the trunk of the car and handing back the change. The couple, as you might expect, was very grateful.

The woman posted the story on social media and in no time at all it had been viewed millions of times and became a national news story. "Most people I know would have done the same thing I did," the woman responded when asked about her act of giving. "I was just in the right place at the right time. Offer to help anyone you can. Not everyone has someone to turn to."[2]

Give Your Ear

We have one mouth and two ears, and we should all try to use them in that proportion more often. That is especially true in times of adversity. Sometimes our friends, our families, or our coworkers need a place to express their frustration, anger, and sadness or simply to talk out how to handle a problem. They don't necessarily need us to solve anything for them as much as they need us to listen.

When Claire Levin stopped to talk with me that summer morning, she listened more to what I *didn't* say than to what I did say. She was curious and empathetic, her attention focused entirely on me. I came to learn this was a way of life for her; she was always "listening" for ways she could intervene.

Give Your Life Experience

As we move forward in our lives and successes come our way, our past experiences sometimes fade from our memories. It's hard to remember that we were once an uncertain freshman in high school, had a first nervous day on the job, or had anxiety when our first baby came home. The passage of time denies us the intensity of those moments, when so much hung in the balance. Yet there are others in similar stages of their own life journeys who need to know that we too had those feelings once. The pain of our past can be a present-day reality for someone else. Sharing our life experiences, our testimony rather than our advice, can often help others navigate their own.

Give Items You No Longer Use

One way to give to others is to give items you no longer use. This can come in the form of clothes, furniture, appliances, or old computers and laptops. Many organizations like the Salvation Army, Goodwill, and Habitat for Humanity make this easy to do; they will come right to your home to pick up your used items. This frees up some space or helps declutter your home. At first glance these objects appear to be simply material things that have outlived their usefulness, and you may be glad to be rid of them. You don't know where—or to whom—those items go from there. You don't get to see how the person who gets those items uses them, nor do you see the meaning they might have for that person's life.

This was true for the books Claire Levin brought me. When I finally sat down with her all those years later, I was able to tell her how much the books meant to me. In turn, she described how the books came to be in my possession. She and Fred often purchased books for their three boys, but with specific instructions. When the oldest was done with a book, he was to pass it on to the next until all of them had read it. They were also always to treat the books well while they were in their possession. The books were to be placed in a box on the front porch. One time when they protested going through such a painstaking process, she responded in a firm, motherly tone, "Why, do you need them anymore?" What the boys did not know was that when the box became full, she would bring them to me and did so for well over a decade, unaware that the books had become my light.

Give Your Goodness

Giving back to society can take on a lot of different forms. It can mean volunteering in your local community or making charitable contributions to a cause or organization. Giving your time and money are important and necessary, but they're not the only way to make an impact. Another kind of contribution we can make shows up in our everyday interactions. We can give our goodness to another human being: holding a door open, saying hello, addressing them by their name, showing patience in stressful situations, trying to see their point of view, and showing them the same compassion we show our family. We all have the capacity to demonstrate these behaviors in our daily lives. When we do, even in the smallest of interactions, we set in motion a ripple of goodness and positivity that we benefit from as well.

What was so remarkable about Claire's goodness was that she never quite knew the effect of her actions. But for me, her example became a way of *being*, of trying to apply her effect as often as I can in my daily life. One particular time, following that path led to a series of events that I could not have scripted.

A few years ago, I walked into my office in Chicago after a long business trip. On top of a stack of mail was this short letter:

I am a fifth grader at Old Hammondtown School in Mattapoisett, Massachusetts. I have just read your book, *A Chance in the World*. I am very inspired by your story. You showed amazing courage by dealing with the Robinsons. I love how you showed perseverance by trying and trying again to find your original family and pulled through even when times were worst.

You and me are different people but that doesn't mean I can't be inspired by you and that should be the same for everyone else. I have been inspired to just keep trying even though things are bad and things will always turn out to be better. Thank you.

This enterprising young boy had managed to find where I worked, almost certainly using the internet. I couldn't stop smiling as I read the letter, thinking fondly of my elementary school days and my detective skills. But I'd never thought to do something like write to one of my favorite authors, let alone track them down. I needed to acknowledge his letter, but a simple follow-up thank-you letter did not seem sufficient. What if I went to Old Hammondtown School and surprised him in his class? The more I thought about it, the better the idea sounded.

The next morning, I called the school and sought out his teacher, Mrs. Casi. I introduced myself and told her that I had received her student's letter. She was quite surprised I had contacted her; he had not expected to ever hear from me, assuming I would be too busy to reply. At the forefront of my mind in reaching out to him and his school was the memory of the lighthouses my elementary school and my teachers had been to me. This was my chance to be a lighthouse for someone else. Of course, I always had the example of Claire Levin to remind me of the impact that small things could have on a young person's life.

When I shared my idea of surprising the class, Mrs. Casi immediately became excited. As we discussed how we might go about planning my visit, an idea struck her. "What if you talk to the entire school, rather than just his class?" I chuckled quietly and thought, "That's why teachers are so great. When it comes to their students, they will ask for the moon."

"Of course," I responded. I'd be quite honored. Mrs. Casi now just needed to get permission from her principal. She said she would do so and get back to me.

She did call back and shared that initially the principal had been reluctant. It wasn't quite the right time, her principal said, and besides, she did not know who I was and had never heard of me. "I'm going to bring his book in for you to read over the weekend," Mrs. Casi told her boss. She stopped by her office, handed her my book, and was halfway through the door when she heard the principal exclaim, "Oh my!" When she turned back around, the principal was shaking her head in amazement.

"How soon can he come?" she asked.

Mrs. Casi was puzzled. "I don't understand. You said yesterday that the time wasn't right." She gestured at the book in the principal's hand. "Don't you want to read that and learn a little bit more about him?"

The principal looked up, still holding an expression of surprise. "I'm sure I'll learn a lot more about him from read-ing this. But a lot of it I already know."

She paused for a moment. "I was his second-grade teacher, almost forty years ago."

When the young boy wrote to me, he did not know that his principal, Mrs. Rose Bowman, had once been my teacher. In responding to his letter, I did not know either. The gift of a book had connected me to him in the same way that a similar gift had connected me to a kind neighbor many years ago. I suspect a small part of me was trying to repay the kindness of Claire Levin. In the course of trying to do what one of my lighthouses had once done for me, I also remembered what Claire had said when I asked why she brought me books all those years.

"It was something my mother told me to do," she replied simply. "Give from where you are with whatever you have."

Can't we all?

CHAPTER 10

SETTING YOUR
SAIL FOR HOME

There it is; the light across the water.
Your story. Mine. His. It has to be seen
to be believed. And it has to be heard.
—JEANETTE WINTERSON

We have all had human lighthouses in our lives. When we pause for a moment and look back, we see now how different our own journeys would have been without them. Such reflections fill us with gratitude and appreciation because we recognize that the day their light first touched us is the day our lives changed for the better. Like the physical structures they represent, our human lighthouses keep no record of the lives they have impacted. They do not know the life courses they have corrected or the many navigators whose journeys they have protected. While they don't seek reward or recognition for what they've done, we remain in their debt.

Certainly, these humble spirits are often in our families, and that is as it should be. Other times they are found as we walk through the course of our everyday life. Perhaps it was the elementary school teacher who fostered in you a love of learning, a coach who pushed you to be better than you thought you could be, a friend who held your hand in a moment of crisis, a colleague who offered you advice on a career path, or a manager who took a chance on you. When we look harder, we can see that these human lighthouses are all around us, these seemingly ordinary people simply going about their everyday lives. They deliver our mail, teach our children and grandchildren, prepare our food, and check us in at the doctor's office. But in their ordinariness, they have something extraordinary to teach us.

The lighthouse effect is found not only in the people we meet but also in moments that matter. At first glance, these moments appear to be random and disconnected, but in fact they set off a series of events that bend the arc of a life. A conflicted ski instructor gazes down into a valley and finds the clarity to return to his true calling as a teacher. A kind woman heeds the wise words of her mother and delivers a box of books to a despondent young boy. A woman gets on a train and shares a chapter of her life with a complete stranger who walks away with a better understanding of forgiveness. A brave young man draws upon his childhood wish to be a firefighter and saves lives. Grieving families honor their loved ones despite devastating loss, lighting a pathway of healing for others.

Each day is an invitation to seek, and to be, a lighthouse. The light we desperately long to see in the world already exists in us. Wherever you are, however you are—strong and resolute, scared or scarred, uncertain yet still hopeful, perhaps in the midst of your own storm—you have the capacity to be a lighthouse. It is my great hope that you will connect to your own human lighthouses and offer them a further word of gratitude. Most importantly, I am equally hopeful that the future will find you standing on the lantern deck of your own lighthouse, gazing bravely out to sea, summoning the sailor toward safe harbor. As you do, you will be reflecting the wisdom that is as timeless as the structure itself:

Your life is a lighthouse.

ACKNOWLEDGMENTS

Writing a book is never a single-person endeavor, and I am beyond grateful for the village that surrounded me with support. That begins with my wife, Tonya, and our children, Quinn and Vaughn and Kennedy. Thank you for the gift of your presence in my life. Each day with you is a lighthouse effect unto itself.

I have a particular debt of gratitude to the people whose stories I have told in this book: John, Monica, Rajeev and Aisha, Greg, Carmen, Rick, FL and Judy, the Levin family, the Crowther family, and the Peete family. You opened your hearts and homes and shared the extraordinary walks of your lives with me. You've touched me in ways that are impossible to describe, and though I tried valiantly to convey your impact in these pages, I suspect I will still fall a bit short. I will find some comfort in knowing that readers will be as inspired by your lives as I have been.

Thank you to Raoul Davis of Ascendant Group Branding for your partnership over the years and my agent Leticia Gomez of Savvy Literary Services for helping bring this book forward. I am particularly appreciative of the

Zondervan publishing family and in particular Andy Rogers, who understood the spirit of this book and made sure we stayed on mission.

Lastly, I've learned that when you share your story, it provides others the opportunity to do the same. The idea of this book began as a seed when you, fellow travelers, shared your stories with me at conferences, speaking engagements, and on social media. The lighthouse effect really exists because of you. Your light will always shine brightly.

NOTES

Preface

1. *The Lord of the Rings: The Two Towers*, directed by Peter Jackson (Burbank, CA: New Line Cinema, 2002).

Introduction

1. Steve Pemberton, *A Chance in the World* (Nashville: Thomas Nelson, 2018), 204.
2. "The Lighthouse Directory," Ibiblio.org, last updated March 13, 2021, https://www.ibiblio.org/lighthouse/.

Chapter 2: RJ

1. Autism Speaks, *Autism and Health, A Special Report by Autism Speaks*, July 2018, https://www.autismspeaks.org /science-news/autism-and-health-special-report-autism -speaks.
2. "Autism Statistics and Facts," Autism Speaks, accessed March 16, 2021, https://www.autismspeaks.org/autism-statistics.
3. Peete family, in personal communication with the author, summer 2020.
4. U.S. Bureau of Labor Statistics, *Persons with a Disability: Labor Force Characteristics*, February 24, 2021, https://www.bls.gov/news.release/disabl.nr0.htm.
5. Charles Duhigg, *The Power of Habit: Why We Do What We*

Do in Life and Business (New York: Random House, 2014),
loc. 1046 of 6093, Kindle.

6. The Los Angeles Dodgers won the 2020 World Series. The
   COVID-19 pandemic prevented RJ from being with the
   team that season, but he was still presented with a World
   Series ring.

Chapter 3: FL Kirby

1. "Mission," Norwich University, accessed March 16, 2021,
   https://www.norwich.edu/about/1212-mission-statement.
2. Online Etymology Dictionary, s.v. "encourage," accessed
   March 16, 2021, https://www.etymonline.com/word
   /encourage.

Chapter 4: Greg Anthony

1. U.S. Citizenship and Immigration Services, s.v. "orphan,"
   accessed March 16, 2021, https://www.uscis.gov/tools
   /glossary/.
2. "Orphans," United Nations Children's Emergency Fund, June
   16, 2017, https://www.unicef.org/media/media_45279.html.

Chapter 6: Carmen Ortiz-McGhee

1. Henry David Thoreau, *The Journal: 1837–1861*, ed. Daimon
   Searls (New York: New York Review Books, 2009), 65.
2. Daniel Patrick Sheehan, "Death on Parade: How the
   1918–20 Influenza Pandemic Ravaged Philadelphia
   and Terrorized the Lehigh Valley," *Morning Call*,
   September 21, 2019, https://www.mcall.com/news
   /local/mc-nws-spanish-flu-1919-lehigh-valley-deaths
   -20190921-qhwt2kvjqzgpfhkesw2myb2ie4-story.html.

Chapter 7: Welles Remy Crowther

1. "Men and Women for Others," Religion Wiki, accessed
   April 15, 2021, https://religion.wikia.org/wiki/Men_and

_Women_for_Others#:~:text=On%20July%2031%2C%20
1973%2C%20the%20feast%20day%20of,become%20
the%20foundational%20element%20of%20Jesuit%20
education%20worldwide.

2. Jim Dwyer et al., "Fighting to Live as the Towers Died," *New York Times*, May 26, 2002, https://www.nytimes.com/2002/05/26/nyregion/fighting-to-live-as-the-towers-died.html.

3. Katie Walmsley, "9/11 Anniversary: Survivor Reflects on Escaping Death," ABC News, September 9, 2011, https://abcnews.go.com/US/September_11/911-anniversary-survivor-reflects-escaping-death/story?id=14479161.

4. Welles Remy Crowther Charitable Trust, accessed February 19, 2021, https://www.crowthertrust.org/.

Chapter 8: Monica Kachru and Rajeev Tipnis

1. "About Anaya," Anaya Tipnis Foundation, accessed February 19, 2021, https://anayafoundation.org/.

2. "International Suicide Statistics," Suicide.org, accessed March 16, 2021, http://www.suicide.org/international-suicide-statistics.html.

Chapter 9: Claire Levin

1. Steve Pemberton, *A Chance in the World* (Nashville: Thomas Nelson, 2018), 33.

2. Caitlin O'Kane, "Woman Helped Elderly Couple Get Food When They Were Too Scared to Go Shopping During Coronavirus Outbreak," CBS News, March 13, 2020, https://www.cbsnews.com/news/coronavirus-elderly-rebecca-mehra-twitter-buys-couple-groceries-scared-to-go-into-store-during-oregon-outbreak/.

A Chance In the World

An Orphan Boy, a Mysterious Past, and How He Found a Place Called Home

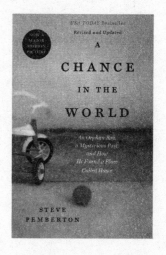

A Chance in the World is the astonishing true story of a boy destined to become a man of resilience, determination, and vision.

Taken from his mother at age three, Steve Klakowicz lives a terrifying existence. Caught in the clutches of a cruel foster family and subjected to constant abuse, Steve finds his only refuge in a box of books given to him by a kind stranger. In these books, he discovers new worlds he can only imagine and begins to hope that one day he will find his true home.

A fair-complexioned boy with blue eyes, a curly Afro, and a Polish last name, he is determined to unravel the mystery of his origins and find his birth family. Armed with just a single clue, Steve embarks on an extraordinary quest for his identity, only to find that nothing is as it appears.

A Chance in the World (Young Readers Edition)

An Orphan Boy, a Mysterious Past, and How He Found a Place Called Home

In this Young Readers Edition, *A Chance in the World* teaches children:

- to begin each day with hope
- that there is goodness in the world, and it is possible to be a beacon of light for others
- that they can overcome challenging circumstances
- that everyone comes from different backgrounds and has value
- to apply Steve's inspirational message to their own lives, through age-appropriate discussion questions

Available in stores and online!